Career Decisions

Albert Richard
Wisconsin Indianhead College, Rice Lake, Wisconsin

Dr. Gary Searle
University of Wisconsin–Stout

DELMAR PUBLISHERS INC.™

I(T)P

NOTICE TO THE READER

Cover design by Spiral Design

Delmar staff:

Acquisitions Editor: Mary McGarry
Project Editor: Theresa M. Bobear
Production Coordinator: James Zayicek
Art & Design Coordinator: Douglas Hydelund

For information, address Delmar Publishers, Inc.
3 Columbia Circle, Box 15-015
Albany, NY 12212-9985

Printed in the United States of America
Published simultaneously in Canada
by Nelson Canada,
a division of the Thomson Corporation

1 2 3 4 5 6 7 8 9 10   XXX   00 99 98 97 96 95 94

Library of Congress Cataloging-in-Publication Data

Richard, Albert.
    Career decisions / Albert Richard, Gary Searle.—1st ed.
        p.   cm.
    Includes index.
    ISBN 0-8273-5993-4
    1. Job hunting—United States.   2. Career development—United
States.   3. Applications for positions.   I. Searle, Gary.
II. Title.
HF5382.75.U6R53   1994
650.14—dc20
                                                                93-40056
                                                                     CIP

TABLE OF CONTENTS

Preface

As a job seeker in today's job market, you will be facing numerous questions and challenges. For example, did you choose a career that matches your skills, abilities, interest, and goals? Are you prepared and educated in the appropriate job-seeking skills? Can you write a personal resume and letters of application and follow-up that meet professional standards? Have you mastered good interview techniques? Are you aware of employer expectations once you begin your job? Do you know what sorts of behavior can get you fired in today's sensitive work environment? This text-workbook will help you answer these questions and meet the dual challenges of career decisions and job application.

As a result of many years of experience in education and business, your authors have incorporated into *Career Decisions* the best and most updated information possible concerning careers, job application techniques, and job success traits. As you work through this text, you will develop knowledge and skills that will give you an important advantage, or extra edge, over others applying for the same job. Our goal in writing this book has been to provide you with both a skills-based text for your course use and a handy reference guide for use throughout your work years. We hope our advice benefits you today and in the years ahead.

CONTENTS

Career Decisions is divided into eight distinct chapters and topics. Chapter 1, "Occupational Planning for the 1990s," will help you to analyze the factors that are needed to make a career decision. You will also learn to discover and utilize essential resources in helping you to search for job possibilities. In addition, this chapter will focus on identifying occupations with the most growth potential and opportunities for the 1990s and beyond.

Chapter 2, "The Personal Resume," will help you to prepare the sort of effective resumes that get you interviews. Emphasis will be on resume formats, structure, and information about the type of applicant that employers are seeking. Integral to this chapter are examples of effective resumes for different occupations.

Chapter 3, "The Cover Letter," will prepare you to write the sort of professional job application letter that should always accompany your resume. Topics covered include the purpose of a cover letter, making a good first impression, where to use your cover letter, and the development of a successful cover letter and letter of inquiry. In addition, the chapter will provide guidelines for both general letter writing and for writing cover letters specifically.

Chapter 4, "The Job Application Form," will offer an entire chapter's worth of information concerning this all-important step in the job hunting process. This chapter will identify both the information you must have and the techniques you will need to fill out a job application form correctly and completely. Of special emphasis in this chapter is a detailed explanation of the sections of the job application form that you have to fill out prior to your job interview.

Chapter 5, "The Job Interview," will focus on the information and preparation necessary to get ready for a successful job interview. Subjects covered in this chapter include the importance of the interview, ways of preparing for your interview, and types of interview questions. Also emphasized in this chapter is the importance of your personal characteristics and personal appearance, as well as information concerning pre-employment testing, and what steps to take after completing your interview.

Actions to be taken once your interview has been completed are covered in Chapter 6, "After the Interview." This chapter emphasizes the importance of the post-interview self-evaluation and preparation of the thank-you letter, in addition to providing examples of the thank-you letter, the not-interested thank-you letter, the letter acknowledging a job offer, the letter accepting a job offer, and the letter declining a job offer. Also covered are the telephone follow-up and the possibility of revisiting the employer after the job interview.

Chapter 7, "Your First Day and Month On the Job," provides important information about coping with your first day and month with a new employer. This chapter offers valuable advice about how to dress and behave on the job, as well as what to do and what not to do.

Finally, in Chapter 8, "Work Ethics," appropriate work behavior is discussed, including ethical issues and sexual harassment. The information in this chapter is designed to contribute to your job success and keep you from being fired.

In addition, two appendices have been included at the back of the text. Appendix 1, "The Psychology of Change," focuses on revising your attitudes toward work to adopt to the new work environment. Appendix 2, "Giving Good Answers to Tough Interview Questions," offers good advice about dealing with sensitive interview questions that you may not have anticipated.

Also included at the back of this book is a glossary of all terms boldfaced and defined within the text. This glossary will serve as a handy reference to students throughout their course of study.

SKILLS DEVELOPMENT

Career Decisions includes three end-of-chapter features to assist you in your review of information covered and your use of skills learned. First, "Questions for Review and Discussion" offers you the opportunity to check your recall of chapter concepts and terminology. Then, "Case Study" presents real-world career situations and allows you to call upon the knowledge you have gained in each chapter to respond accordingly. Finally, the chapter-ending "Project" provides a minds on activity allowing you the opportunity to build the skills you have learned to develop effective resumes, prepare successful cover letters, and so forth.

SPECIAL FEATURE

Also included in each chapter of *Career Decisions* is a feature titled "Expert Advice," which offers valuable information and insightful career advice from experts in the job search field. Among the topics covered in this feature are the psychology of change, resume tips for job seekers, what an employer looks for in a cover letter, the value of the job application form, interviewing from an employer's perspective, and ways to increase your employability.

INSTRUCTOR'S GUIDE

Developed to accompany *Career Decisions,* the Instructor's Guide provides chapter overviews, suggestions for classroom discussions, answers to all chapter review activities, chapter tests, and chapter test answer keys. In addition, transparency masters are included for use as handouts or lecture aids.

Acknowledgments

We would first and foremost like to thank Sheila Furjanic for convincing us to write *Career Decisions*, and Mary McGarry for having the faith in our ability to produce a successful text for Delmar. We would also like to thank Bob Nirkind for all his advice and encouragement and for helping us to develop the first edition of this text.

In addition, we would like to thank the following reviewers, whose suggestions and encouragement throughout the development of this text were greatly appreciated:

- Diane Ewalt, Watterson College Pacific, Vista, California

- Nina Newberry, Tulsa Technology, Tulsa, Oklahoma

- Carrie Grider, Southside High School, Selma, Alabama

Furthermore, we would like to thank Mary Schiller, Nancy Vrieze, Laurie Gargulak, Wisconsin Indianhead Technical College, and the University of Wisconsin-Stout for their advice and support. Also, we would like to thank Carol Richard and Maxine Searle for their help and support.

Bert Richard
Gary Searle

About the Authors

Gary Searle is currently a professor of marketing education at the University of Wisconsin-Stout where he has also held administrative positions as program director for marketing education and department chairman for Communications, Education and Training. He was formerly a state supervisor for marketing education in Wisconsin and Tennessee. Previously, he taught marketing education at the high school and vocational-technical college levels in Milwaukee.

Dr. Searle received degrees from Austin Peay State University, the University of Wisconsin-Whitewater and the University of Tennessee. In addition to holding leadership positions in education, business, civic and church organizations, he has authored over forty publications and done consulting in such diverse places as Belize, Wales and Nigeria. In 1992, he received outstanding teacher and best research presentation awards.

With eleven years of full-time occupational experience, Gary Searle has been involved in sales, retailing management and real estate. He holds a Wisconsin real estate broker's license, and he and his wife, Maxine, just completed building their twelfth home. Additionally, they have found time to enjoy traveling to all fifty states and 49 foreign countries. They have two children, Michael and Mary Ann.

Albert Richard is currently an instructional supervisor at Wisconsin Indianhead College-Rice Lake, Wisconsin. Previous to his current position, he was former program director and assistant professor of marketing education at the University of Wisconsin-Stout. Prior to UW-Stout, Mr. Richard was a marketing teacher-coordinator at Superior Senior High School, Superior, Wisconsin. He also has several years of retail sales and management experience in the appliance business.

Mr. Richard received his bachelor's degree in Marketing Education from the University of Wisconsin-Stout, a master's degree in Business Education from UW-Superior, and his specialist degree in Vocational Education from the University of Wisconsin-Stout.

In the past ten years, Bert Richard has been president of the Chamber of Commerce, Rotary Club, Wisconsin Administrator's of Business and Marketing Occupations, local Men's Club, and a local youth baseball association. He has taught several classes and seminars in job application, customer service, marketing, and management. He is married to Carol Richard and has one son, Jon Richard.

CHAPTER 1

Occupational Planning for the 1990s

OBJECTIVES

After completing this chapter, you should be able to:

1. Identify the best occupations for the 1990s and beyond.
2. Evaluate your learning potential with educational preparation and experience.
3. Match your job skills, abilities, interests, and education with a potential career.
4. Identify techniques that are useful in searching for potential employers.
5. Explain and cope with job hunting stress.

YOUR CAREER PATH: POSSIBILITIES AND POTENTIAL

You may have heard this statement many times before: "I wish I knew what I want to be when I grow up." Or: "If I had to do it all over again I would be a . . . ." Or this familiar question: "So what are you doing after graduation?" If you do not know the answer to this question, you are among millions who are in the same boat. Do not feel bad; there are people in their forties or fifties who are still looking for the answers.

Obviously many high school and college students are trying to find their career paths. So do not get frustrated or feel lost and alone. Just be patient; we hope this book will help you to meet the challenge of finding an appropriate career or job.

One word of caution. Finding a career may be a challenge you will encounter more than once in your lifetime. Most people change careers four to six times during their work lives and change jobs within those careers eight to ten times before they reach age 40. Thus, the process of looking for a career is usually not a one-time experience.

What is really scary is that career counselors and employment experts are telling us that many of the jobs that are present today will either change or be eliminated by the year 2000. In addition, the experts are saying that 75 percent of the occupations in the United States will require not only a high school education, but at

Graduating from school is only the first step in entering the world of work. The better prepared you are for the process of determining a career and seeking a job, the better your chances of a fulfilling and successful work life. (Photo by Ron Jawarski.)

least another one or two years of education, especially in a technical skill area. Furthermore, about 25 percent of the occupations in this country will require a four-year university degree at the minimum.

Before we assess your career abilities and opportunities, let us look at what occupations will give you the best chance for landing a career.

OCCUPATIONAL TRENDS FOR THE 1990s

You should be aware that there are several factors that will influence occupational trends in the future. These factors include:

- **The size and composition of the labor force.** With the aging of the baby-boom generation, more than a third of the population will be forty-five years of age or older by the year 2005. Predictions also indicate that there will be more women and minorities in the work force in managerial as well as administrative positions.

- **Educational background.** What many people may not realize is that the jobs requiring more education are also the jobs growing the fastest in today's economy. In other words, the more education you have, the better chance you have of getting a job. In addition, the more education you have, the better income you can expect. The current median income for a high school diploma is $18,902; for 2 years of college, the median is $21,975; for a college degree, the median figure is $31,029.

- **Environmental issues.** Many technical jobs on city, state, national and international levels will be required in order to deal with the problems of pollution, air quality, water quality, garbage, ozone, and chemical and industrial wastes.

Where the Workers Are Employed

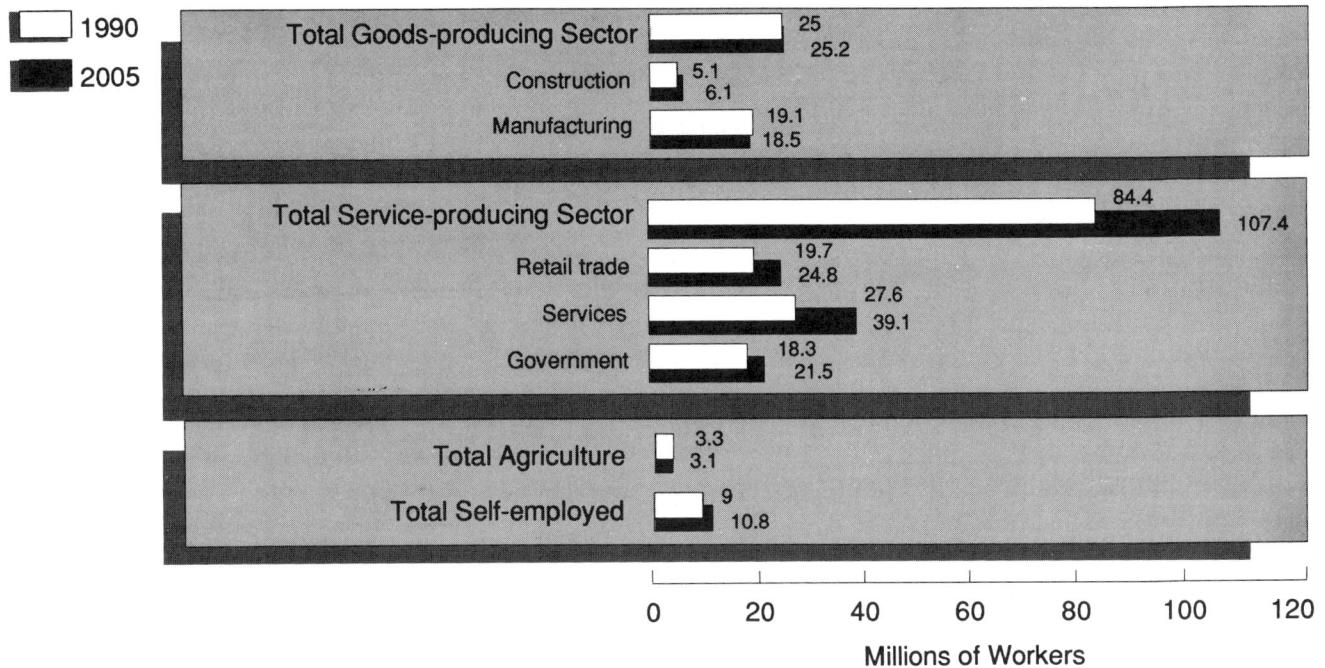

| | 1990 |
| | 2005 |

Total Goods-producing Sector — 25 / 25.2

Construction — 5.1 / 6.1

Manufacturing — 19.1 / 18.5

Total Service-producing Sector — 84.4 / 107.4

Retail trade — 19.7 / 24.8

Services — 27.6 / 39.1

Government — 18.3 / 21.5

Total Agriculture — 3.3 / 3.1

Total Self-employed — 9 / 10.8

0   20   40   60   80   100   120

Millions of Workers

Figure 1-1. (*Source: Vocational Education Journal,* February 1992)

- **Economic conditions and related conditions.** The long-term shift from goods-producing to service-producing employment is expected to continue. The national debt, the balance of trade, recession cycles, interest rates, political policies, and employment trends will have a significant impact on various careers. Changing technology and business practices, increased foreign competition, and shifts in the demand for goods and services will reshape tomorrow's workforce.

- **Demographics.** Projections by the Bureau of the Census indicate that the West will continue to be the fastest growing region of the country, increasing in population by about 19 percent between 1990 and 2005. Elsewhere, the South will increase by 15 percent, the Northeast will increase by 4 percent, and the Midwest will remain about the same. What may be a "hot" job in the Midwest may not even exist in the western states, and *vice versa*. An occupation that is paying a great salary in Dallas, Texas may be paying a terrible salary in Milwaukee, Wisconsin.

Two of the best sources for occupation and career information are *The Occupational Outlook Handbook,* published by the U.S. Department of Labor, Bureau of Labor Statistics; and *The Dictionary of Occupational Titles,* published by the U.S. Department of Labor, Employment and Training Administration. These are excellent sources for job seekers who need current, accurate, and comprehensive career information about workers' job descriptions, necessary training and education, earnings, working conditions, and future job prospects. Let us now look at the specific occupational trends for the 1990s.

Service Occupations. By the year 2000, nearly four out of five jobs will be in the industries that provide services (see Figure 1.1). These jobs will be in such occupations as banking, health care, education, computers and data processing, and management consulting. The fastest growing jobs will be:

1. Service jobs within corporations and governmental agencies (state and local government jobs will rise faster).

2. Legal and business services (advertising, accounting, word and information processing, and computer support).

3. Retail trade, especially in the food and drink area, grocery stores, department stores, and miscellaneous shopping goods stores (sporting goods, jewelry, books, cards, and stationery).

Goods-producing occupations. Most of these occupations, especially in manufacturing, will remain constant or decline. Construction is the only occupation expected to show an increase, but only in the business and commercial sectors. Manufacturing areas that may show increases in jobs include electronic computing equipment, medical instruments and supplies, some plastic products, and printing. The decline in agricultural and mining jobs will continue into the year 2000.

Professional/technical occupations. The growth in the service sector will also create jobs for engineers, accountants, lawyers, nurses, and many other managerial, professional, and technical workers. The fastest growing occupations will be those that require the most educational preparation. The occupations within this group include:

1. Natural, computer, and mathematical scientists (computer and data processing, genetics, lasers).

2. Health diagnosis assessment, and treatment occupations (registered nurses, physical therapists).

3. Technical occupations (engineering, health, and scientific assistants, legal assistants, and computer programmers).

4. Professional service (medical/dental assistants, protective services, and cleaning).

5. Engineers (electrical and environmental).

6. Marketing and sales (real estate agents, brokers, travel agents, securities and financial services, and retail managers).

7. Managerial occupations (health service managers).

8. Professional specialists (lawyers, social scientists, and social workers).

9. Teachers (pre-school and elementary).

10. Repair services (mechanical and electronic).

11. Administrative support (secretaries, data entry, word processors, and accounting assistants).

12. Transportation (aircraft pilots and flight engineers).

The Fastest Growth Rate Jobs. Between 1990 and 2005, the Bureau of Labor Statistics predicts that employment will rise from 123 million to 147 million jobs. (Table 1-1 indicates the fastest growing occupations.) This prediction was made with some degree of accuracy based upon occupations with training and strict entry requirements. However, since most occupations have several methods of entry and, at times, flexible requirements, the potential supply of workers is difficult to measure. Thus, shortages and surpluses are sometimes hard to predict.

Table 1-1. Fastest Growing Jobs Growth Rate, 1990–2005

Home health aides	92%
Paralegals	85
Systems analysts	79
Personal aides	77
Physical therapists	76
Medical assistants	74
Operations research analysts	73
Human services workers	71
Radiologic technicians/technologists	70
Medical secretaries	68
Medical scientists	66
Physical therapy aides	64
Psychologists	64
Travel agents	62
Correction workers	61
Data processing equipment repairers	60
Flight attendants	59
Computer programmers	56
Occupational therapists	55
Management analysts	52
Medical equipment repairers	51
Child care workers	49
Information clerks	47
Legal secretaries	47
Marketing, advertising, p.r. managers	47
Podiatrists	46
Registered nurses	44
Therapists	44
Nursing aides	43
Restaurant cooks	42
Health technologists	42
Licensed practical nurses	42
Preschool teachers	41
Private detectives	41
Producers, actors	41
Gardeners	40
Special education teachers	40

Source: "Outlook: Where the Jobs Are" by Kathy Leftwick, *Vocational Education Journal*, February 1992. Copyright 1993, The American Vocational Association. Reprinted by permission.

One factor to remember when checking the outlook for an occupation is that growth in employment is only one source of job openings. In fact, most openings arise out of the need to replace workers who transfer to other occupations or leave the labor force. As a result, even occupations with slower than average growth, may offer many jobs for new workers, especially if large numbers of people work in them.

Occupations With the Most New Jobs. Service-producing industries—including transportation, communications, and utilities; retail and wholesale trade; services; government; and finance, insurance, and real estate—are expected to account for approximately 23 million to 24.6 million new jobs created by the year 2005. In addition, the services division within this sector—which includes health, business, and educational services—contains sixteen of the twenty fastest growing industries. Expansion of service sector employment is linked to a number of factors, including changes in consumer tastes and preferences, legal and regulatory changes, advances in science and technology, and changes in the way

OCCUPATIONAL PLANNING FOR THE 1990s   COPYRIGHT © DELMAR PUBLISHERS INC.   **5**

Table 1-2. Occupations Adding the Most Jobs by 2005

Retail sales worker	+887,000
Registered nurses	+767,000
Cashiers	+685,000
Office clerks	+670,000
Truck drivers	+617,000
Executives, managers	+598,000
Nursing aides	+552,000
Waiters, waitresses	+449,000
Secondary school teachers	+437,000
Information clerks	+422,000
Systems analysts	+366,000
Child care workers	+353,000
Gardeners	+348,000
Accountants	+340,000
Computer programmers	+317,000
Elementary school teachers	+313,000

Source: "Outlook: Where the Jobs Are" by Kathy Leftwick, *Vocational Education Journal*, February 1992. Copyright 1993, the American Vocational Association. Reprinted by permission.

Job Educational Requirements

These jobs require a bachelor's degree or more education:	**These jobs require education beyond high school:**	**These jobs require no more than high school graduation:**
• Systems analyst/computer programmer	• Paralegal	• Home health aide
• Physical therapist	• Radiologic technician/technologist	• Human service worker
• Operations research analyst	• Medical assistant	• Personal aide
• Psychologist	• Physical therapy aide	• Correction officer
• Computer programmer	• Data processing equipment repairer	• Travel agent
• Occupational therapist	• Medical records technician	• Flight attendant
• Management analyst	• Surgical technician	• Retail salesperson
• Marketing, advertising and public relations manager	• Restaurant cook	• General office clerk
• General manager/top executive	• Respiratory therapist	• Cashier
• Teacher	• Licensed practical nurse	• Food counter, fountain worker
• Accountant, auditor	• Maintenance repairer	• Truck driver
• Lawyer	• Teacher aide	• Nursing aide
	• Registered nurse	• Waitpeople
	• Legal secretary	• Information clerk
	• Medical secretary	• Gardener/grounds-keeper
		• Guard
		• Child care worker
		• Secretary
		• Clerical supervisor
		• Stock clerk, floor sales

Figure 1-2. (*Source: Vocational Education Journal*, February 1992.)

businesses are organized and managed. Table 1.2 identifies the ten occupations with the most new jobs.

YOUR EARNING POTENTIAL

According to the *Vocational Education Journal* (February 1992), the more education a job requires, the higher the salary. You should realize that the jobs requiring more education are also the jobs growing the fastest in today's economy. As mentioned previously, some jobs require a one-year or two-year post-secondary degree, while others require a college degree. Nearly all jobs call for a high school degree (see Figure 1-2).

For all occupations, the median annual income is $21,543. For jobs that require a college degree, that figure is $31,029. With one to three years of college, the income is just above the median level at $21,975. With a high school diploma, the annual income figure is $18,902. Without it, the median is only $15,249.

Within specific occupations, the difference in earnings potential is more dramatic, as shown in Figure 1-3. In the health care field, for example, health service workers (orderlies, attendants, and aides), who typically have only a high school diploma, earn a median weekly salary of $263. Among technologists and technicians, who usually have some post-secondary training, the median weekly salary is $398. For health assessment and treatment occupations (dietitians, pharmacists, registered nurses, and therapists), most of which require a college degree, weekly earnings are $600. In health diagnosing occupations (physicians and other medical specialists), where education beyond a four-year college degree is required, the salary is $824 a week.

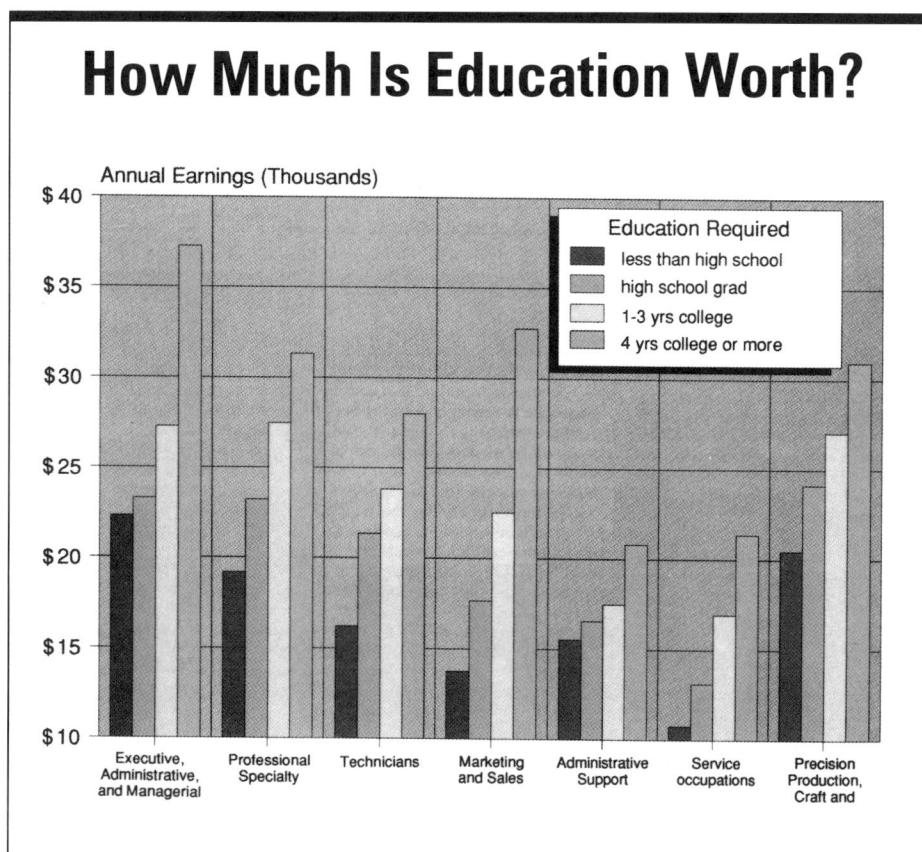

Figure 1-3. (*Source: Vocational Education Journal,* February 1992.)

Table 1-3. Self-employed Occupations with Above-Average Job Growth from 1990–2005

Psychologists	76.5%
Social scientists	63.1
Gardeners	50.6
Management analysts	47.1
Child care	45
Managerial	33.9
Artists	32.9
Cosmetologists	26.4
Painters	35.0
Electricians	29.3
Secretaries	25
Adult instructors	25
Vocational teachers	25

(*Source: Vocational Education Journal*, February 1992.)

SELF-EMPLOYMENT

More than ten million people now claim to be self-employed in the United States. From sales people to construction workers, their numbers will continue to grow by nearly 1.5 million in the next fifteen years.

Most self-employed individuals tend to be sales workers, but the greatest growth in self-employed workers has been, and is expected to continue to be, in executive, managerial, and administrative occupations. These individuals are usually entrepreneurs who choose to start new businesses.

Another major segment of the self-employed sector is service, which includes workers ranging from barbers to electricians. Significant growth is expected among self-employed child care workers, gardeners, painters, electricians, and cosmetologists (see Table 1.3).

EXPERT *Advice*

A SURVEY OF BUSINESSES RANKS TOP FIVE JOB SKILLS

Job searches can be difficult enough without trying to second-guess what the employer is looking for in a new hire. Also, the corporate climate changes constantly to keep pace with the economy and needs of individual businesses.

With that in mind, Celestine Schall, director of career development at Alverno College, believed a positive and realistic way to keep current was to visit a variety of area businesses and government agencies. Her goal was to discover firsthand what employers were seeking in job candidates and to obtain practical advice on how people should market themselves.

"Today, employers are really focusing on the need for communication. Twenty years ago, people would talk about [job candidates] being prepared within the field and knowledge base. Now they are saying that preparation within the area is still very important, but you must have the communication abilities to operate within the occupation."

She lists the "top five" criteria that employers look for in job candidates: communication skills, initiative and enthusiasm, appearance, ability to solve problems, and responsibility/flexibility.

Not surprisingly, excellent communication skills headed that list.

"Employers are looking for communication ability across the board—speaking with others, being able to write, being able to be a team member in order to help people think through plans with other people and get ideas, being able to deal with multi-cultural populations, dealing with top CEOs

Celestine Schall

and government officials as well as communicating effectively with any person who may walk through the door."

Second, Schall said employers want people who are enthusiastic and show initiative, those who are interested in what is happening. "The company wants to know what the interviewee can do for the corporation, how well the person will contribute," she said.

Appearance ranked third on the list; companies want their employees to present a good image and to be promotable. "It isn't just clothes, but self-assurance—how the person presents himself or herself," Schall said.

Fourth, employers are seeking people who have good problem-solving ability.

"In an interview, you must support what you are saying with examples and use your experiences intelligently to support their abilities," Schall said.

Finally, employers value responsibility and flexibility.

Schall also emphasized the importance of the resume and cover letter in showing writing skills so an employer can screen you "in" rather than "out."

ASSESSING YOUR CAREER OPTIONS

Now that you have a good idea of what the "hot" jobs and careers are going to be in the years to come, you need to look at your life style, personal characteristics, strengths, traits, weaknesses, and goals. The next step in your career-seeking process is to develop a "career plan."

DEVELOPING A CAREER PLAN

A career plan is like a map that will lead you to your ultimate destination: a career or job at which you enjoy working. Your career plan will consist of several steps: assessing your interests, assessing your skills, matching careers with your interests and skills, matching your education with your career interests, developing strategies for finding employment, and identifying additional resources.

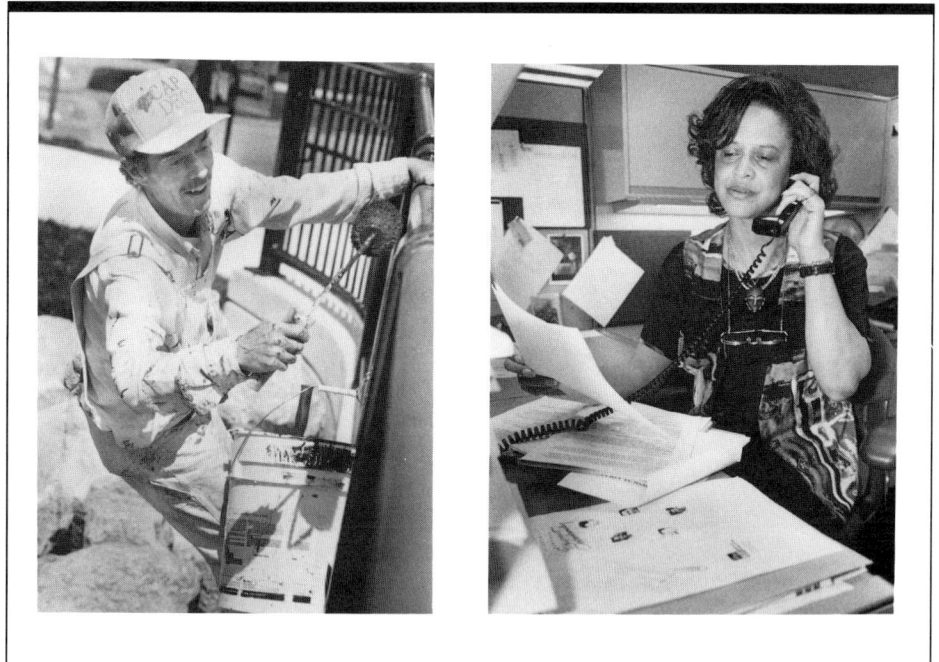

The career you choose should reflect both your interests and your skills. Some individuals prefer working indoors in a professional environment, for example, while others prefer working outdoors in more physically demanding occupations. (Photos by Mary Langenfeld.)

Assessing Your Interests.   The first step in developing a career plan is to assess your interests. What really interests you? What hobbies do you have? What is your life-style? Where do you want to live? Where do you want to work—indoors or outdoors? What size company do you want to work for? Do you want to go into your own business? What is more important—what sort of salary you expect or the kind of work you would like to do? What type of working conditions would you prefer? Jot down your answers to these questions on a clean piece of paper and proceed to the next step.

Assessing Your Skills.   The second step in developing a career plan is assessing your skills. What special skills do you possess? Are you adept in the basic skills—grammar, mathematics, and spelling? How are your communication skills—listening and speaking? Do you have good people skills? Do you have good technical skills, and if so, what are they? In what school subjects did you do best? What subjects in school were your worst? Are you creative, and if so, in what areas? Again, jot down your answers and proceed to the next step.

Matching Careers With Your Interests and Skills.   The third step involves matching careers with your interests and skills. Do any of your answers above match up with any of the occupations listed earlier in this chapter? What are the occupations and careers that come close to your answers? If you find a match, or several matches, jot them down. At this point you should go to *The Occupational Outlook Handbook* and *The Dictionary of Occupational Titles* and read about the career(s) you have chosen. These books are available at any public library or school library. Now go to the next step.

Matching Your Education With Your Career.   The fourth step in assessing your career options consists of matching your education with your career interests. Do you have the right educational background for the career(s) you have chosen? Did you major in the appropriate subject area? How much education is needed to get the job you want in the career you have chosen? In what sort of career can you further your education? What educational background will you need—a specialized course or program, a one-year diploma or certificate, a two-year program or an associate degree, a four-year college or university degree, or a master's or doctorate degree? Jot down your answers and proceed to next step.

Developing Strategies for Finding Employment.   The fifth step to developing your career plan involves identifying strategies for finding employment. Once all your interests, skills, and education are matched up, you need to design an action plan to find employment in the career or job you have chosen. The next section of this chapter will help you develop techniques and methods to achieve your career goal.

Further Career Identification and Exploration.   Finally, if you are still unsure what you would like to do for a career, don't panic! There are many other resources available to you.

1.   Check with local technical schools and colleges or universities to see if they have career development centers. Talk to a career counselor. See if you can take a career or vocational interest test (you can't pass or fail this test). Usually there is a small fee.

2.   Go to your public library and survey several books or articles on careers. The back of this book will provide some references.

3. Check with local employment services. They may offer you some valuable guidance, and usually do not charge for this service.

4. Check with your college or local high school guidance counselor. These individuals usually have updated information and are willing to help.

EXPERT *Advice*
CAREER PLANNING 101

by Jeffrey Landsman

Spring has arrived! I know it's difficult for us to believe that with the continuing cold weather and the blizzard of 1994 still fresh in our memories. But, looking at the calendar, we know it must be spring.

Our desire for change is never stronger than this time of year. We yearn to shed our heavy winter coats and other vestments for lighter, more comfortable garments. To get out and start playing golf, working in the garden or any activity, so long as it is outdoors.

A career move is much the same. We are either tired of what we have been doing, or we look forward to what is next. We look forward to a change. Just making a change, however, is not always what we need. Sometimes, it is direction and purpose that we lack. Seeing, or more appropriately, realizing that is another matter.

Our careers, like aircraft carriers, take a while getting to their cruising speed and are difficult to navigate. Once they are on their way, however, they require some time and thoughtful planning to redirect. Similarly, they contain a contingent of varied "men and material" that have multiple purposes and uses.

My father once told me that my reputation was all that I truly possessed and that I, alone, was responsible for its' content. So is your career. If you strictly decide on emotion alone to determine a career change, you could be making some mistakes.

A career is or should be a natural progression of an individual's work-related experiences and expertise. Careers are extensions of people's aptitude, and abilities defined by success in the work place, on a job or to an industry.

In times past, "the company" made or broke our careers. A person's career was something passive, something that just happened. Many of us rarely had a chance to be proactive in our careers. Today, with different philosophical views of the world relating to an individual's freedom and "happiness," we have a different attitude towards a career.

A successful career brings recognition, respect, power and economic freedom. As is the case with minorities and women, a career is a way to obtain social equality and economic freedom. No longer content with outdated traditional social mores and economic strata, minorities and women have reshaped our thinking by proactively establishing and directing their careers.

So, how does all of this affect you? Good question? You need to decide a few things before you can start the process. Honest self-analysis is absolutely crucial when answering the following questions. First, what do I really want to do? Second, what am I qualified to do? Third, am I willing to pay the price that it will cost to get what I think I want?

What do I want to do? What are my abilities? What are my values? Could what I want conflict with my values? My interests? Will the job fulfill them or merely take up time?

What am I qualified to do? Do I do a good job at my current place of employment? How does what I want to do coincide with my past experiences? What type of natural progression is there?

Am I willing to pay the price? Is there something about the hours or money or work environment that is distasteful to me? Will my family be supportive? What will I have to give up?

 11

So, let's sit down and come up with a general list of job characteristics and rate them from 1 through 5 with one being not important, two being slightly important, 3 being somewhat important, 4 being quite important, and 5 being crucial.

We also need to come up with an ability profile to determine a true picture of ourselves. What are our strengths and weaknesses? Our rating will be 1 far below average, 2 below average, 3 average, 4 above average, and 5 outstanding.

Finding out the truth of what you "really want" is paramount in designing your career. Finding out is never too late, but it is a good idea to be "true to thyself," so as not to waste effort and time. Unlike our reputations, we never possess time. It just keeps ticking away.

Job Characteristic	Important Rating
Salary	_____
Challenge and Responsibility	_____
Friendly Co-Workers	_____
Promotion Opportunity	_____
Job Difficulty	_____
Geographical Location	_____
Job Security	_____
Training	_____
Personal Growth	_____
Travel	_____
Opportunity To Help Others	_____
Schedule	_____
Decision Making	_____
Benefits	_____
Company Reputation	_____
Title	_____
Independence	_____

Ability Profile	Rating
Intelligence	_____
Leadership	_____
Motivation	_____
Direction	_____
Self-Confidence	_____
Energy Level	_____
Self-Knowledge	_____
Competitiveness	_____
Creativity	_____
Perseverance	_____
Initiative	_____
Goal Achievement	_____
Willingness For Responsibility	_____
Interpersonal Skills	_____
Ability To Handle Conflict	_____
Sensitivity	_____
Communication Skills	_____
Flexibility	_____
Organizational Skills	_____
Public Speaking Skills	_____
Persuasiveness	_____
Plus add any job specific skills such as accounting, selling, etc.	_____

(Source: *Food Service News,* June 1993. Reprinted with permission.)

WHERE TO LOOK FOR JOBS

You will soon discover that many jobs are not advertised and that some have not yet been created. Thus, it is important to develop a source bank that will allow you to become a successful job seeker.

The two most important ingredients in your job seeking skills are *initiative* and *creativity*. **Initiative** is the ability to be proactive in seeking potential employers. It is the constant effort to use the techniques and methods you are about to learn in your job seeking efforts. It is definitely not sitting around waiting for employers to call. **Creativity** is the ability to devise strategies and methods to get an interview and land a job. These strategies and methods exploit all the career-seeker's resources, such as networking, publications, employment agencies, educational institutions, and the company or business (Figure 1.4).

NETWORKING

In this case, **networking** is defined as your opportunity to connect with people or groups so that they can assist you in obtaining a job. Either call or write the following people to let them know that you are looking for employment, and to explain what type of job you are seeking:

- Friends (business and social)
- Relatives
- Schoolmates
- Teachers or counselors
- Professionals (doctors, dentists, lawyers, and clergy)
- Former employers
- Social, civic or business organizations

Make sure to keep track of the people you contact so you can tell a potential employer who referred you. Contact as many people as possible.

PUBLICATIONS

There are several publications that can give you an idea of what employment opportunities are available, or provide you with names and addresses so you can make a contact. These publications include:

- **Newspapers.** Morning, evening, and Sunday editions. Sunday editions usually offer the most comprehensive job listings. A word of caution: in many instances only 15 percent of available positions are advertised in the newspaper. You should seek other job sources. (See Figure 1.5.)

- **Trade Publications.** Almost every career is associated with some form of trade journal. Check with local companies, businesses or libraries. They may be able to provide want ads or addresses where you can make job contact.

- **Telephone directories.** The Yellow Pages can give you a good resource for contacting area companies and businesses.

EMPLOYMENT AGENCIES

A serious job seeker will register with both private and state employment agencies. The two most often used are:

- **State Job Service.** You should always register with Job Service because some companies will only hire through this agency.

 13

50 Ways To Learn About & Get Jobs

Successful job campaigns identify the best potential employers and search out information on their job openings. Too many candidates for employment rely on only a few sources of information and may fail to obtain the best job possible. Here is a list of 50 resources which may help to identify employers and jobs—most job seekers should be able to augment this list with a dozen or so by using their own special contacts.

Use Personal Contacts

Family	Fellow job seekers, share leads	Christmas card list
Friends	Mentors, senior level contacts	Former teachers & counselors
Neighbors	Your sports contacts	Ask people you usually cite as references
School or college associates		

Use Employment Related Contacts

Fellow employees	Bulletin board job postings	Former employers
People you worked with on past jobs	"Information interview" ask employers for advice and leads	Ask people who turned you down for a job for leads

Work with Services that Provide Job Leads & Referrals

Guidance/counseling offices	Women's centers	Federal job centers
Library career centers	Job or resume banks	State & local government civil service commissions
Placement services	Professional association services	Convention placement centers
State employment offices	Over 40 counseling services	

Use Published Sources for Employer Information & To Learn of Job Vacancies

Chamber of Commerce directories	Newspaper classified ads	Professional magazine ads
Study financial pages of newspapers to learn of new business ventures	Check ads in old newspapers & magazines to identify employers in your field	Check telephone book "yellow pages" to spot smaller organizations

Obtain Leads from Specialized Reference Books & Periodicals (Illustrative List)

The College Placement Annual	The National Job Market	Career Guide to Professional Associations
National Business Employment Weekly	The National & Regional Job Bank (books)	How to Get a Job in Chicago & How to Get a Job in Dallas/Fort Worth
The Professional & Trade Association Job Finder	900,000 Plus Jobs Annually	

Make Direct Contact with Employers

Unsolicited letter of application and resume	Place want ads for yourself	Use volunteer, unpaid, and temporary or part-time work to get a foot in the door
Walk-in contacts	Telephone job search	
Campus interviews	Job fairs & employer open houses	

Figure 1-4. (*Source:* Courtesy of University of Wisconsin-Stout Career Planning and Placement Center.)

- **Employment Agencies.** Some agencies require a fee for providing job leads. However, many employment agencies now charge the company or business for finding an employee. You will find a listing of employment agencies in the Yellow Pages.

404 *Employment Opportunities*

Excavating Equip. Operator for basement excavation. 555-2276

GENERAL LABOR
Growing eastside company needs 50 workers! Work available on all three shifts
NOW!
8, 10 or 12 hour shifts in factory warehouse and assembly. Bonus program for people with cars. Apply today work tomorrow at:
THE WORK CONNECTION
1047 Evanston
555-9675

General ● Students ●
●● SUMMER WORK ●●
Entry level, PT/FT, all areas. Accepting applications Memorial Day! 555-6459, 18+ ok

General
MACHINE OPERATOR
$6/hr 1st shift short term. Some exp on machines. Prescreened by TFH, TC 555-4342

HARDWARE CLERK
EXPER'D. Must be knowledgeable in electrical, plumbing and general hardware. Must have a good rapport with people. 555-8899

Hotel
HOUSEKEEPING
The Sunwood Inn has immed. openings for Housekeeping. Shifts include wkends & wkdays. Apply in person at 1010 Western Blvd.

INDUSTRIAL
Great Long term position available 1st shift. Possible permanent position, $6/hour to start. Deburring experience preferred, but will train a hard worker. Call Gail 555-7811
PRO STAFF
PERSONNEL SERVICE
Equal Opportunity Employer

Industrial/Light Summer help wanted. $5.50/hr. Apply Register Resale/Tech Svcs, see Jim Johnson 555-0383

INSULATION HOPPER FEEDER NEEDED. 555-7510.

Insurance
Approver/Customer Service
Due to new business, multiple benefit approver/customer service positions avail. at $10/hr. 4 mos. PT training afternoons. FT day positions with complete benefit package after successful completion of training. Keyboard skills nec. Apply in person, Cigna, 5500 Ocean Dr., suite 100, IGH, 555-1036 EOE

JANITORIAL PT
Floor person, exp., 3-7pm M-F. Also avail. - Days PT Summer Only. 555-2340.

JANITORIAL FT, 11PM-6AM, THE OSTEEN HOUSE INN, 555-8883

404 *Employment Opportunities*

JANITORIAL PT-Midway, Rsvi & SE Mols areas. Early eves. Mon-Fri 555-1685

Laborers
BARGE CLEANERS
APPLICATIONS TAKEN AT 40 State St, btwn 8am-2pm, June 2, 3, & 4 ONLY. Company paid physical + drug test req'd.

$6.00 & UP LANDSCAPING. START A.S.A.P.!!!
Several area locations. Must enjoy working outside, be clean cut and have valid drivers license and steel toed boots. Bring picture I.D. and S.S. card. Apply at:
THE WORK CONNECTION
1047 Evanston
555-9675

MANAGEMENT
GLAMOUR SHOTS
High Fashion Photography
We're growing and need your management experience and skill! We have openings in the Minneapolis area for store manager. We offer excellent compensation, benefits, outstanding growth potential and we care about people - they are the heart of our company. Successful candidate must be sales-oriented, a motivated people leader, and committed to great customer service in a retail setting.
Salary potential: $30-$60K/yr.
Submit resume to:
Human Resources
4455 West 23rd, Suite 209

Management
ON-SITE APT MANAGER
Exper. & ref. req. Aggressive marketing skills a must. Salary negot. Send resume to CSP Apts., 555-0800

★ MANAGER ASSISTANT ★
Convenience store, fuel & auto wash complex. Afternoon & eve/wknds. Good start pay, benefits, some C store exp. Call Don 555-7810

Management
Looking for 10 Managers & Asst Mgrs. to help us expand our co. If you are young at heart & are interested in your future, not your past, call Leonard 555-1902

MEAT PACKING
DAYS OR EVES
25 full time workers needed for 1st or 2nd shift. Will train. Immediate openings in south metro area. Bonus program for people with good attendance and for people with cars. Great potential. Apply as soon as possible at:
THE WORK CONNECTION
1047 Evanston
555-9675

404 *Employment Opportunities*

MECHANIC
SCHOOL BUS & TRANSIT
Exper preferred. Exper w/ I.H. and Detroit Diesel & Spicer Trans., electrical systems. Class A license preferred. Competitive wage and benefit package. Contact Ken 555-9290.
COMFORT BUS CO.
Equal Opportunity Employer
Pre-employment drug screening req'd.

MECHANICS
FT Experienced fleet mechanic for 2nd shift. Midway location. Must have own tools. Uniform furnished Health & vacation plan. National, 555-1959, EOE.

MEMBER SERVICE REP, FT, Postal Credit Union, Related experience required. Apply or send resume to: 2401 Maple Rd, attn: Jeanine.
Equal Opportunity Employer

Metal fabrication
SAW OPERATOR & SHEAR OPERATOR, 555-1568

MILLWORK
Immediate opening in window & door shops for person with basic carpentry skills. Millwork or lumber yard exp high desirable. Apply in person at Mutual Door, 2655 Richfield Rd

MONOGRAMMER, FT or PT, eves, to run computerized mach., exp pref but will train. 555-3624

Motorcycle
SUMMER HELPER
555-2168 DAN
PAUL'S HARLEY-DAVIDSON
949 Atlantic Ave

ORDER TAKER/CLERK
If you a people person & don't mind spending time on the phone, requirements include 1yr PC exp & typing 50wpm. Exc benefits including health, dental, life & retirement plan. Apply at 1140 Broadway
EOE/AA

PRINTER
DP/COUNTER PERSON
Must be comfortable working with computers & have DP knowledge. Versatility is a big plus; printing knowledge a must. Efficient work habits are nec. Should enjoy communicating with clients & co-workers. Fast-paced, young, aggressive company. Future mgmt. positions possible. Call Mike, 555-2026

RECEPTIONIST
FT position beginning 03-05-94. Responsibilities includes answering 12 incoming lines with 80 extensions, processing incoming and outgoing mail, typing, and other misc. duties.
Qualifications required in-

404 *Employment Opportunities*

clude: 1-2 years experience on similar size phone. Accurate typing skills on word processor. Professional people skills, good organization skills-ability to handle many duties simultaneously. A very upbeat and positive attitude.
If you meet these qualifications, please fill out an application at Cedars Clinic, 3060 Elmont Road. Before 5:00 p.m. February 3.

RECEPTIONIST, PT
Manufacturing firm seeking friendly professional individual to work afternoons 12-5pm M-F at our active reception desk. Exp w/busy phone system required. Task flexibility a must. Need someone who is responsible & works well under pressure. Resp for 8 incoming lines & 22 extensions. Additional hrs may be avl. Smoke-free environment. Please contact Sue at:
ALL-PURPOSE WIRE & CABLE
1835 Ellis Park Dr
555-1800

RENTAL AGENT
Work weekends & vacations, $6 per hr. 555-0078

Restaurant
RESTAURANT MANAGERS
At Eat 'n Run, fun and profits go hand in hand.
It is profitable to have fun, especially if you are involved in a multi-million dollar restaurant operation with fun as the main ingredient. We offer quality service, casual dining atmosphere, and fine spirits. But providing "fun" is our main attraction.
We are opening new restaurants in 1993, and to meet our expansion goals we are seeking Managers who have a minimum of two (2) years full-service restaurant management experience and are anxious to meet the expansion and growth opportunities available with Eat 'n Run
We offer excellent salary and benefits.For consideration, send resumes only - no phone calls please.
Restaurant Associates, Inc.
5700 Doppler Dr., Suite 115
Attn: Sue Anderson
EOE M/F

Restaurant
HOST/HOSTESS
For new Sports Bar that's opening. We need a Host/Hostess (Floor manager) Full Time and also PT to fill in on days or eves. Apply Before 11am or After-2pm
Steve's 1560, Big Bear Ave

Restaurant
FOOD SERVICE
Experienced cooks, cashiers, utility/dishwasher, prep positions available. Mon-Fri, Call 555-5134. EOE.

Figure 1-5. Classified Advertisements

EDUCATIONAL INSTITUTIONS

If you graduated from a college or university, the best place to make contact is the institution's placement office. Many listings, especially if they are related to the programs and majors of the college or university, come through the placement services of the institution. Business and industry also contact former teachers, professors, and counselors for employee leads. Make sure you contact them.

THE COMPANY OR BUSINESS

Making a personal contact with a business may help you to get an idea what is available. You can arrange a visit or write to the human resource department (sometimes referred to as the *personnel department*), where you would apply for a job in a large company. In smaller businesses or companies with few employees, the owner or manager is the person responsible for hiring. [REMEMBER, YOU SHOULD ALWAYS FIND OUT ABOUT A COMPANY OR BUSINESS BEFORE YOU APPLY FOR A JOB THERE.]

COLD CALLS

Another job-seeking method that could help you find a job is the door-to-door or "cold call" method. Once you have identified what type of employment you are seeking and have identified potential employers, you then make an unannounced visit to the employer's place of business. There are several questions you should ask:

- Do you have an application form?

- Is there someone I could talk to about potential job openings?

- Are job openings handled by the company or an employment service?

- To whom in the company should I send my credentials (resume, application blank, application letter, references, and transcripts)?

Again, remember to dress as if you were going to be interviewed. The receptionist or secretary may be in charge of initially screening candidates, so you want to be as pleasant and professional as possible.

JOB HUNTING STRESS AND FRUSTRATION

A few words need to be said about job hunting stress. It can result from a long lag time between interviews, a lack of employer response, employment refusal, or resource exhaustion. Some of the symptoms are fear, doubt, lack of self-esteem, and financial worries. Most experts agree that there will always be some stress in job hunting, but point out that small amounts of frustration and stress can cause you to be more productive and more aggressive. Here are some helpful hints in dealing with job hunting stress and frustration:

- **Attitude.** Keep your emotions and mind on an even keel. Engage in activities that make you feel good. Practice positive thinking.

- **"Friend Uppers".** Talk to a friend or relative who will give you some positive strokes.

- **Humor.** Do not let your sense of humor be jeopardized by stress. Humor is a good stress reducer.

- **Physical Activity.** Develop or continue some sort of physical routine. Lag time is a good time to keep fit, and fitness does reduce stress.

SUMMARY

Finding a job is a challenge that you will encounter more than once in your lifetime. Most people change careers four to six times during their work lives and change jobs within those careers eight to ten times before they reach age 40. The first steps to finding a job, of course, are to know what sources you are looking for, and to try to avoid being impatient and frustrated.

Occupational trends for the 1990s may be categorized into three areas:

- *Service occupations* such as banking, health care, education, computers, data processing, and management consulting.

- *Goods producing occupations* such as electronic computing equipment, medical instruments and supplies, plastic products, and printing.

- *Professional/technical occupations* such as engineering, accounting, law, and nursing.

The more education a job requires, the higher the salary. While nearly all jobs call for a high school diploma, the more education the job requires, the greater the income you can expect to earn.

More than 10 million Americans claim to be self-employed, with a growth of nearly 1.5 million anticipated in the next fifteen years. Although most self-employed individuals tend to be salespeople, the greatest growth is in executive, managerial, and administrative occupations, as well as in service occupations.

Once you have decided what career areas you might be interested in, there are six steps to developing a career plan:

- Step 1: Assessing your interests

- Step 2: Assessing your skills

- Step 3: Matching careers with your interests and skills

- Step 4: Matching your education with your career interests

- Step 5: Developing strategies for finding employment

- Step 6: (Optional) Further career identification and exploration

There are a number of effective methods and sources to use in looking for a job:

- Networking

- Publications

- Job Agencies

- Educational Institutions

- The Company or Business

- Cold Calling

Job hunting stress and frustration can occur when there is lag time between interviews, a lack of employer response, employment refusal, or resource exhaustion. The symptoms include fear, doubt, lack of self-esteem, and financial worries. You can deal with job hunting stress and frustration by doing the following:

- Keep your emotions and mind on an even keel; engage in activities that make you feel good, and practice positive thinking.

- Talk to a friend or relative who will make you feel more positive.

- Keep your sense of humor.

- Develop or continue some sort of physical activity.

QUESTIONS FOR REVIEW AND DISCUSSION

1. Mike Smith is going to school to learn a technical trade. He is worried that what he is learning will be outdated by the time he graduates. Should Mike worry?

    _____

    _____

    _____

    _____

2. You have heard that jobs in Alaska really have high salaries. If you are planning on a career in this state, what should you investigate before you move there?

    _____

    _____

    _____

3. Of all the occupations listed as the top careers for the 1990s, what occupations might be affected by changes in the environment?

    _____

    _____

    _____

4. Take the average salary of any of the top occupations and divide that salary by fifty-two weeks, and then divide again by forty hours to arrive at an hourly rate. What hourly rate did you arrive at?

    _____

    _____

5. Name two important job sources published by the United States government and explain where you can find them.

    _____

    _____

    _____

    _____

6. Why do you think employers are sometimes reluctant to advertise for jobs in the newspaper?

    _____

    _____

    _____

7. You have heard it said that many job openings go unadvertised. How do employers find out about potential employees?

    _____

    _____

    _____

8. In this chapter you were told that it is important to learn about potential companies or businesses before you apply. Why is it important?

_____

_____

_____

9. In most large companies, what department does most of the hiring? In small companies, who does the hiring?

_____

_____

_____

10. If you were to write a prescription for combating a disease called job stress, what would that prescription be, or what would its ingredients be?

_____

_____

_____

_____

CASE STUDY

Etan Schwartz just graduated from a two-year technical college where he majored in marketing. Since graduation, only two jobs in marketing have been posted in his college placement office. Both jobs required Etan to move from his current city. In addition, there have been no marketing jobs advertised in the local newspaper for months. Etan thinks his college placement service stinks and does not think much better of the local newspaper. What do you think his problem is? If you were Etan's career counselor, what advice would you give him? What options can you suggest to him?

PROJECT

Using the career profile outline below, pick three careers you would like to investigate. One career should be something that is beyond your wildest imagination. The second career should be one that you think suits your skills, abilities, life-style, and educational goals. Finally, pick a career that you never heard of. Report your findings to your class.

CAREER PROFILE

NAME OF CAREER: _____

_____

_____

CAREER DESCRIPTION: _____

_____

_____

REQUIREMENTS: _____

_____

_____

_____

_____

ADVANCEMENT: _____

_____

_____

_____

_____

EDUCATION AND TRAINING: _____

_____

_____

_____

_____

FUTURE OUTLOOK: _____

_____

_____

_____

_____

The Personal Resume

After completing this chapter, you should be able to:

1. Explain what a resume is and describe how it can help you in the career search process.

2. Discuss the latest trends in resume preparation.

3. Identify the important content areas of a resume.

4. Describe the differences between chronological, functional, and combined resumes.

5. Select a resume format that will effectively highlight your personal and professional experiences.

6. Prepare a job resume.

DEFINING THE RESUME

Resume is a French word that means "a short history of one's life." Since there is no agreement on the proper punctuation of the word, you may use *resume* (most common), *resumé, résume,* or *résumé.* A resume, pronounced *rez-a-may,* is sometimes referred to as a personal data sheet or vita. While the terms are used interchangeably, *resume* is most common in the business world, especially at the management level.

A **resume** is basically an organized outline of information that is relative to your getting the job you want. In effect, it is an advertisement for yourself. Properly created, it can greatly enhance your chances of landing the job you want. Incorrectly done, it will ensure that you will fail in your attempt to get the position you desire. The resume serves as the required foundation on which to build a structure of strong and effective employment search skills. A strong resume is absolutely necessary in your quest for the position you desire, because finding a good job in the nineties is an extremely competitive task.

THE PURPOSE OF A RESUME

The primary purpose of a resume is to provide a prospective employer with the information necessary to consider interviewing you. A resume and cover letter (to be discussed in Chapter 3) are often the first contact you have with a prospective employer, thus emphasizing the importance of this component in your job search. First impressions are lasting impressions, and you do not get a second chance at making a good first impression. Therefore, it is critical to build a solid foundation in your job search by creating a quality resume.

USING YOUR RESUME

Since the resume is an essential tool to your job search, it can be used in a number of ways. First, the resume and cover letter are sent together and work hand in hand in providing vital information to the prospective employer. A cover letter is simply a letter to the prospective employer stating what position you are interested in, and providing information not outlined on your resume that is pertinent to the employer. In effect, it is a sales letter that complements your "advertisement."

Providing a resume and application letter is usually the first step you take when pursuing a specific job. If you are successful in creating a favorable first impression, the employer will respond by contacting you, usually by mail or phone, and ask that you complete a job application form. If you are unsuccessful, an employer will usually, but not always, send you a rejection letter.

Second, you can use your resume when completing a job application form. As previously mentioned, your resume is an outline of important facts detailing your qualifications for a job; these facts are usually requested on application forms. Your resume will serve as a handy guide to use in completing this form in a thorough and accurate manner.

Third, a copy of your resume should also be brought with you to your interview. Since it is possible that you will be interviewed by more than one person, or that the interviewer may not have a copy of the resume you sent, providing one at the interview will create a favorable impression by demonstrating your organizational ability.

EXPERT *Advice*
RESUME TIPS FOR JOB SEEKERS

Jerry Esposito is the Human Resources Manager for Sears' home office in Chicago, Illinois. In this capacity, he reviews and evaluates hundreds of resumes a year as a first step toward filling open positions and adding new employees to the company. As an experienced personnel manager, Esposito has plenty of good tips to share for preparing effective resumes.

The first thing Jerry Esposito recommends that a job seeker do in developing a solid resume is to have a focused career objective targeted to the specific industry, and, where possible, to the specific company in which the applicant is interested. For example, if you want a career as a buyer, your career objective might include being a "senior carpet buyer for Acme Carpets, Inc." rather than simply "a buyer for a large or small retail organization." While the former objective tells the employer that the applicant is interested in a specific job with a specific company, the latter objective indicates that the applicant has a "canned" resume and is probably looking for any kind of job with any company. For a company like Sears, where they like to hire people who know what they want and are focused on achieving their career aspirations, the resume that appears "canned" would most likely not lead to an interview.

Job stability is also an important consideration to Jerry Esposito. In reviewing resumes that cross his desk, he looks for applicants who have shown upward mobility—in responsibilities, promotions, etc.—in previous jobs. In Esposito's eyes, stability has less to do with your staying with the same company for a number of years than it does with demonstrating that you have a meaningful, specific career progression.

To ensure that an employer will have your resume on hand for your interview, be sure to bring an extra copy along with you—just in case. (Photo by Mary Langenfeld)

Form is important to Esposito as well. While he prefers to review one-page resumes, he fully accepts that some individuals require a two-page resume if they have had a number of career moves. Esposito stresses that the extra space which you gain by preparing a two-page resume should be used to highlight significant information regarding your accomplishments with previous employers.

This lead Esposito to emphasize the importance of clarifying all statements regarding accomplishments and achievements. As an example, he asks you to consider the following statement from a resume he received: "Outstanding Salesperson." What does this statement tell you? Does it tell you what product was sold, or when it was sold, or how many salespeople there were, or how sales were measured? Now consider this statement: "Outstanding Salesperson—Sold over three million dollars of roofing materials in 1993 to lead a nine-person sales staff." Much clearer, isn't it? This additional explanation clarifies the applicant's achievement and allows the employer to understand just how outstanding he or she was in the job.

Finally, a tip from Jerry Esposito for job seekers who have been convicted of a felony. Esposito suggests you do not include this information on your resume, as it may hurt your chances of getting an interview and proving your job worthiness. He recommends that you save this information until you have been called for a job interview, when you can ask if this presents a problem to the company and state that you would like the opportunity to explain your past situation. In such a situation, honesty prior to the first interview may help you win the job you seek.

TRENDS IN RESUME PREPARATION

When writing your resume, you should keep in mind the following current trends in resume preparation:

ONE–PAGE LIMIT

In most cases, a one-page resume is recommended. If organized correctly, you can get the information necessary to create the desired impression on a single page. Very seldom should you use more than one page, because busy employers will not take the time to read it. A long, drawn out resume may cause an employer to question your creativity, organizational ability, or even your self-esteem. A two-page format should be used only when you have considerable experience and skills relative to the specific job for which you are applying and the position is a professional one in nature. In this case, you may want to expand on your experience and/or skills to show prospective employers you have the qualities they are seeking.

LIMITED PERSONAL INFORMATION

You need only to list personal information on your resume that will be beneficial for a specific position. Due to federal and state anti-discrimination laws, certain personal information is illegal for an employer to ask. Therefore, it is not necessary to list:

- gender
- age
- birthplace
- height
- weight
- condition of health
- marital status
- number of children
- religion
- race
- social security number

Specific examples of personal information you *should* include on your resume will be discussed later in this chapter.

ACTION-ORIENTED ACHIEVEMENTS

You should emphasize your abilities and experiences through action-oriented statements rather than statements of fact. In keeping with many traditional resume formats, you may list your work experience as shown in Figure 2.1.

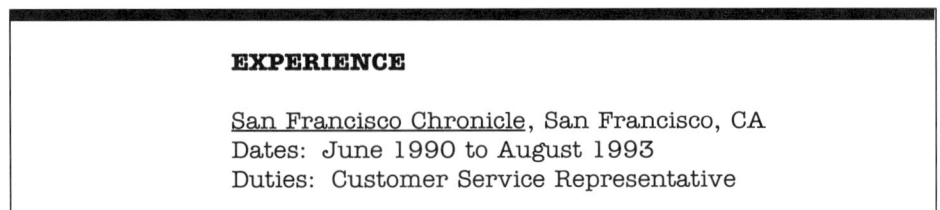

EXPERIENCE

San Francisco Chronicle, San Francisco, CA
Dates: June 1990 to August 1993
Duties: Customer Service Representative

Figure 2.1. Resume Excerpt: Using Statements of Fact

However, the description of work experience in Figure 2.1 does not really effectively emphasize the job seeker's abilities or achievements. To make your resume more action-oriented, this section could be revised to use the format shown in Figure 2.2.

```
┌──────────────────────────────────────────────────────────────┐
│                                                                │
│  EXPERIENCE                                                    │
│                                                                │
│  Customer Service Representative                               │
│  San Francisco, Chronicle                                      │
│                                                                │
│  * Created solutions in the customer complaint department      │
│       Developed telephone skills reacting to challenges        │
│       presented on a daily basis.                              │
│       Excellent problem solving in dealing with irate          │
│       customers in a professional and diplomatic manner        │
│       under pressure situations.                               │
│  * June 1990 to August 1993                                    │
│                                                                │
└──────────────────────────────────────────────────────────────┘
```

Figure 2.2. Resume Excerpt: Using Action-Oriented Achievements

This revised description of work experience provides a much more definitive description of what this individual accomplished in the previous job.

REPLACE POSITION WANTED/CAREER OBJECTIVE

Another trend in the 1990s involves using one or two action-oriented sentences at the beginning of your resume in place of the traditional position wanted/ career objective section. This action-oriented approach is most suitable to management positions that require a variety of job duties. Figure 2.3 is an excellent example of this approach. This powerful, action-oriented statement should be placed at the top of your resume directly under your name and address.

```
┌──────────────────────────────────────────────────────────────┐
│                                                                │
│  PROFESSIONAL TARGET                                           │
│                                                                │
│  Management-level position in a national retailing/wholesaling │
│  company that emphasizes direct responsibility for project     │
│  control, profit and loss and balance sheet project analysis,  │
│  and follow through implementation of strategic goals and      │
│  plans.                                                        │
│                                                                │
└──────────────────────────────────────────────────────────────┘
```

Figure 2.3. Resume Excerpt: Replacing the Position Wanted/Career Objective Section

ELIMINATE ALL REFERENCES TO CAREER CHOICE

Another trend in resume preparation is to eliminate entirely any reference to career choice, including position wanted, career objective, and the action approach. Simply start your resume by listing your work experience, education, and capabilities or achievements. This approach does not focus on any particular job, but it does leave a strong resume open for employer interpretation. Based on the strength of your background, the employer may try to find or create a position for you. This method makes the employer look more deeply into the resume to find your strengths, rather than discarding it because your career objective does not fit into the company's hiring plans.

THE VIDEO RESUME

A new and emerging trend in the job-seeking process involves the use of the video resume. Many professional human resource search firms will make a video of you, for a price, and then send the tape to perspective employers. The highly structured format of a professional video assures you of an excellent product that has a good chance of being seen by employers. Like a telephone interview, the employer can save time and effort by simply viewing tapes of applicants and deciding which three or four people to bring on-site for interviews. In this way the video resume benefits both employer and job seeker.

Some job applicants are now making videos with their own home video equipment. The tapes often begin with the applicant discussing major highlights from the resume, including past professional achievements and accomplishments. Career goals, both present and future, are also emphasized, along with the applicant's educational background. Activities, interests, and hobbies are sometimes mentioned and references are reviewed, with a suggestion to contact the applicant for additional information.

The video resume is a creative and unique way to make a good first impression with a prospective employer, and it is gaining in popularity every day. If you produce your own video resume, however, be sure it is reviewed by other people for quality production and image.

PREPARING YOUR RESUME

Developing an outstanding, hard-hitting resume takes a great deal of time and effort on your part, but the end result is worth it. To begin preparing your resume, you should first collect the information needed relative to the position you are seeking, and then develop a rough draft in a comfortable format. Then, get helpful opinions from knowledgeable individuals, such as teachers, guidance counselors, placement directors, or business people. Don't be afraid to ask for help with your resume.

Finally, prepare your final draft. This process will guarantee a quality finished product.

Typical information needed on a resume includes:

- Personal Information

- Position Wanted and/or Career Objective

- Education

- Work Experience

- Activities, Interests, and Awards

- References

These topics form the outline of your resume. What follows is an explanation of each topic and some appropriate examples.

PERSONAL INFORMATION

Basic personal information that should be provided on your resume includes: 1) your full name; 2) your complete address, including street number and name, apartment number (if applicable), city, state, and zip code; and 3) your phone number with area code. If you are currently attending college and have both a temporary and permanent address, and two phone numbers, you should list them as well. If you will be moving to a new address, simply list the new address as your permanent address, and indicate when the new address will take effect (see Figure 2.4).

```
┌─────────────────────────────────────────────────────────────────────┐
│                                                                       │
│   Present Address:                    Permanent Address:              │
│   309 Cedar Street                    (as of June 1, 1994)            │
│   Provo, Utah 74751                   1919 Augusta Street             │
│   (555) 238-2064                      Ogden, Utah 74868               │
│                                       (555) 836-2132                  │
│                                                                       │
└─────────────────────────────────────────────────────────────────────┘
```

Figure 2.4. Providing Two Addresses on Your Resume

Remember, one of the trends for the nineties is to provide limited information concerning your personal life. Much information cannot be legally asked of you. If you are comfortable providing additional personal information, and feel that it may benefit you in applying for this particular position, use your judgment in including it. For example, if you are applying to Lutheran Brotherhood Insurance Company, and you are Lutheran, include it on your resume, but just for that particular job. It may help you get the position.

Also, be sure all information provided on your resume is complete; eliminate abbreviations so your resume is consistent.

POSITION WANTED

In this section of your resume, you want to indicate a specific position that interests you. Even if you are interested in more than one position, you should not list multiple positions wanted. It is better to completely eliminate this section in this instance. If you list multiple positions, it may give the impression that you are not sure what you want, or that you lack focus. It may also give the impression that you are begging for any job. In listing your position wanted, you should be as brief and specific as possible, to give the prospective employer the impression that you have given some thought to what you would like to do for them. Examples of positions wanted might include:

- Salesperson
- Retail Management
- Secretary
- X-Ray Technician
- Security Officer
- Nurse

CAREER OBJECTIVE

The career objective section of your resume can be used to complement your position wanted section, or it can be used alone if you do not have a specific position wanted. This section should be tailored to fit the particular employer that interests you. An example of how you can complement your position wanted section with your career objective is shown in Figure 2.5.

```
┌─────────────────────────────────────────────────────────────────────┐
│                                                                       │
│            *   Position Wanted:   Salesperson                         │
│            *   Career Objective:  Sales Manager                       │
│                                                                       │
└─────────────────────────────────────────────────────────────────────┘
```

Figure 2.5. Complementing Your Position Wanted With a Career Objective

If the position you are interested in relates to your long-range career plans, as in Figure 2.5, it shows the employer that you have set goals for yourself and that you may be a self-starter. In essence, you have demonstrated a career direction.

As previously mentioned, you may want to eliminate the position wanted section of your resume if there is no specific position that interests you or that you know is available. In this case, you can then develop a broader career objective in order to give the employer a more general idea of your employment goals. Examples of more general career objectives are shown in Figure 2.6.

CAREER OBJECTIVE

* To secure an interesting and challenging career in the field of marketing.
or
* To pursue a professionally gratifying position in the graphic arts industry.
or
* To obtain an elementary education position with involvement in co-curricular activities.
or
* To acquire a fulfilling position with a child care organization.

Figure 2.6. Listing Your General Career Objectives on Your Resume

In each case, the goals in Figure 2.6 are general enough to give the prospective employer an indication that you may be interested and qualified for various positions with the company, but specific enough that the employer has a good idea of the focus of your interest in the organization.

The position wanted and career objective sections should be tailored to specific job openings and particular organizations whenever possible. Make the employer feel that you are focused, and that the company is definitely the right one for you.

EDUCATION

In this section of your resume, you want to list your educational background, starting with the highest level you have achieved to date. List the school(s) you are attending or have graduated from first. Give the date you graduated, or your projected graduation date, and your major area of study. Be sure to list any co-op, internships, or work-study experiences as well. If you have earned any awards or honors, you may include those here too. You do not have to list high school educational experiences, just post-secondary educational activities.

In the event that you do not have a post-secondary education, or did not complete high school, simply list the schools attended and graduation date or years completed. Examples of how to list your educational background are presented in Figure 2.7.

University of Virginia
Charlottesville, Virginia 13892
B.S. May 1994
Major: Marketing Management
Minor: Economics
GPA: 3.28 Dean's list three semesters

Mills Senior High School
Mills, Idaho 09642
Completed two years

Figure 2.7. Listing Your Educational Background on Your Resume

WORK EXPERIENCE

The heart of your resume is your work experience. This is the section that employers who review your resume concentrate on the most. Most employers prefer applicants who have previous work experience, so it is important to highlight your past experiences carefully and in a way that will appropriately advertise your abilities to the prospective employer.

Some specific guidelines in developing the work experience section include the following:

1. List your previous employers in order, with your present or last employer first. In other words, list them in reverse order from when you worked for them.
2. State the name of each business and its location.
3. Provide a short description of your major duties.

There is no absolutely correct format for listing your work experience. Some people choose to list their duties first, followed by the names of their employers. Others choose to highlight their employers first, and then list their duties. It is in this section that you want to be sure to use action-oriented phrases to sell yourself. An example of how to list your work experience is shown in Figure 2.8.

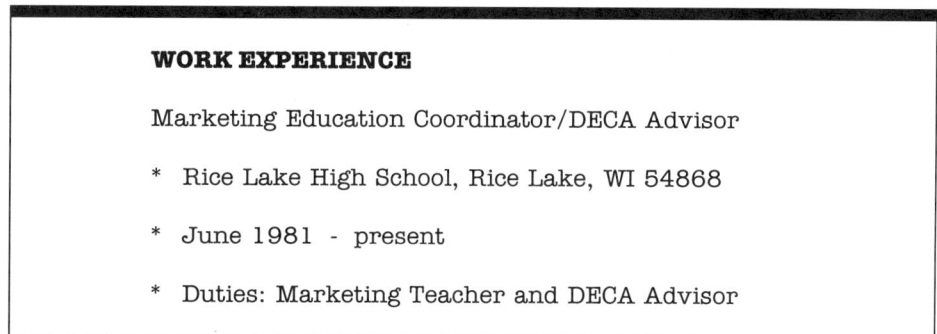

WORK EXPERIENCE

Marketing Education Coordinator/DECA Advisor

* Rice Lake High School, Rice Lake, WI 54868

* June 1981 - present

* Duties: Marketing Teacher and DECA Advisor

Figure 2.8. Listing Your Work Experience on Your Resume

The example in Figure 2.8 follows a more traditional way of listing work experience, but is not action-oriented. Figure 2.9 is a revision of Figure 2.8 with a more action-oriented approach.

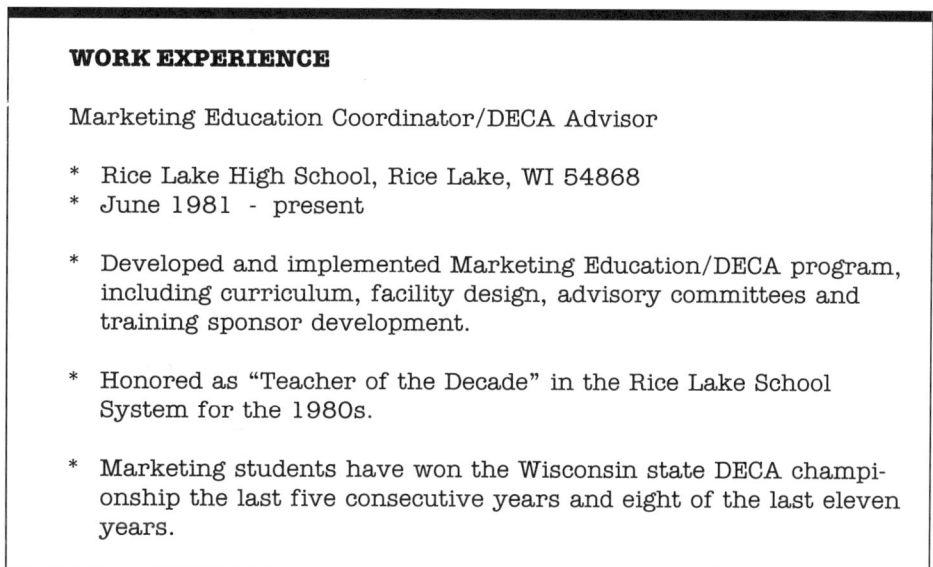

WORK EXPERIENCE

Marketing Education Coordinator/DECA Advisor

* Rice Lake High School, Rice Lake, WI 54868
* June 1981 - present

* Developed and implemented Marketing Education/DECA program, including curriculum, facility design, advisory committees and training sponsor development.

* Honored as "Teacher of the Decade" in the Rice Lake School System for the 1980s.

* Marketing students have won the Wisconsin state DECA championship the last five consecutive years and eight of the last eleven years.

Figure 2.9. Revised Listing of Work Experience With an Action-Oriented Approach

Another approach, using a different order of listing work experience, is shown in Figure 2.10.

WORK EXPERIENCE

<u>Micro-switch Incorporated</u>—Jackson, MS 54751

June 1992 - present

Duties: Training and Development Specialist

Figure 2.10. Another Approach to Listing Work Experience

Again, the example in Figure 2.10 is a more traditional format. You can make this more action oriented by mentioning accomplishments, as shown in Figure 2.11.

WORK EXPERIENCE

<u>Micro-switch Incorporated</u>—Jackson, MS 54751

June 1992 - present

Duties: Training and Development Specialist Developed an
          employee training program for entry level employees
          that cut employee turnover by ten percent and helped
          to increase department sales by eight percent in the first
          year of implementation.

Figure 2.11. Listing Work Experience by Mentioning Accomplishments

You do not have to list every job you ever had. This is especially true of part-time jobs. Forget them unless the job was directly related to the current position you are seeking. Also, if you only have part-time experience, such as summer jobs during school, list them and include your duties just as you would in the full-time listing.

Ten years is a good rule of thumb when deciding how much work experience to list. This chronological list, present position to past, should include any non-paid experiences you may have completed, such as two years in the Peace Corp. This practice will fill in all time blocks in your chronological list. If there are time gaps in your work experience, be prepared to explain them in your job interview. The same is true for time served in prison. An employer can legally ask if you have ever been convicted of any crime, so time served may as well be included in your resume. Another school of thought says to eliminate prison time served from your resume, especially if it was over ten years ago, and deal with this question during the interview, when you can fully explain past circumstances.

After you finish the work experience section of your resume, take a good look at it from an employer's point of view. How does it look? What image of you does it project? Does the list of jobs make you look like a job jumper—someone who has had several jobs in a short period of time? Employers do not like to spend a great deal of money and time training someone, only to have the employee leave before the company gets a return on its investment. Therefore, an employer will be looking at your resume to see if you have changed jobs often. If you have, be prepared to explain your actions.

ACTIVITIES, INTERESTS, AND HOBBIES

You may or may not want to use any or all of these headings, depending on what activities, interests, and hobbies you may have. Be sure to list any that fit the position you are seeking. Employers are interested in people who are active, and this section can highlight your past and current civic, community, and professional involvements. Remember to list any leadership positions you have held, and describe any involvement that emphasizes being part of a successful team. Teamwork is a major trend in business, industry, government, and education in the 1990s.

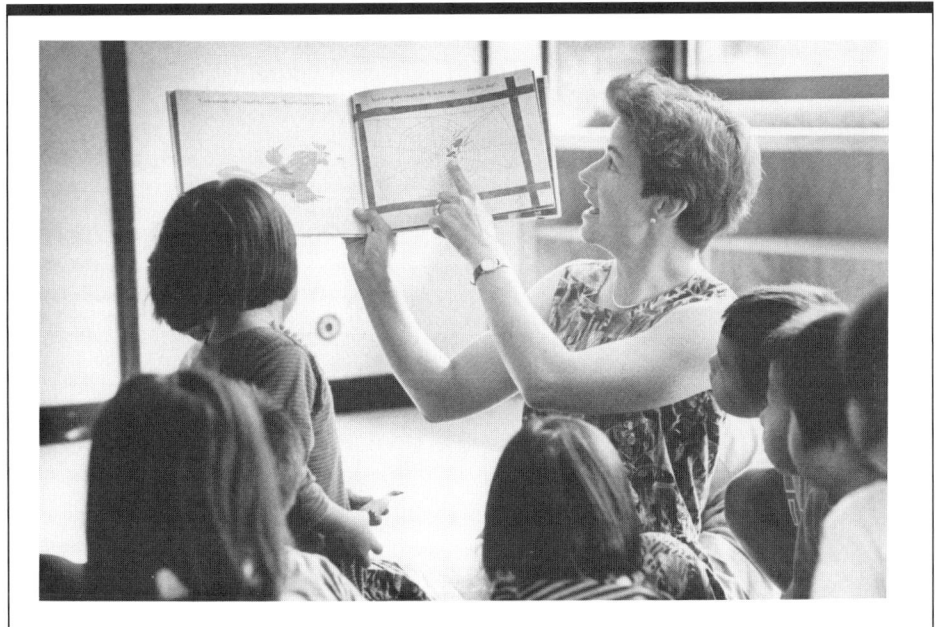

Take advantage of any civic or community work you do in your spare time, or may have done in the past. List these activities under the "Activities, Interests, and Hobbies" section of your resume. (Photo by Mary Langefeld).

It is debatable whether you should list specific personal hobbies. Listing hobbies such as jogging, hunting, softball, and painting does give the employer a more complete picture of your character. However, it is often recommended that you leave this information out and focus on you job-related skills. If you are comfortable listing this information and do not think it will be harmful to your employment chances, go ahead and use it. Controversial hobbies or ones that may be looked at in a negative manner, such as animal trapping or making home-brewed wine, should not be used. Examples of some activities, interests, and hobbies, and their listing in a resume, are shown in Figure 2.12.

```
ACTIVITIES, INTEREST, AND HOBBIES

Kinship Volunteer - Hayward, Ohio
* Have been a Kinship sponsor for an eight year old boy for
  the last fourteen months.
Vice-President - Hayward Jaycees
* Served as Vice President for the last year.
* Served on the Hayward Centennial Committee.
Volunteer Coach - Hayward Recreational Department
* Served as a volunteer basketball coach for fifth and sixth
  grade girls for the past two seasons.
```

Figure 2.12. Listing Activities, Interests, and Hobbies on Your Resume

REFERENCES

References do not need to be included on your resume because employers know that you will furnish references at their request. References are always included on the company application blank, so be prepared to include them at that time, along with their business phone numbers.

If your resume is short, however, complete reference listings are excellent filler. List the names, addresses, phone numbers, and positions of two or three persons who have knowledge of your job experiences and abilities. Using important people as references will add status to your resume. Past and present employers are excellent.

```
REFERENCES

Credentials and references are available by contacting:
Career Planning and Placement Services
Northern Technical College
521 College Avenue
Marquette, Michigan 46821
```

Figure 2.13. Listing References on Your Resume

Teachers, administrators, religious and civic leaders, counselors, and friends who can attest to your character and abilities are permissible. Be sure to get permission from your references before using their names.

Many employers require letters of recommendation from your references, and they may want you to include these letters with your application letter and resume. Some of your references may hesitate to write a letter for you because they are too busy or have never written such a letter before. Some people will even ask you to write your own letter of recommendation, and then they will put it on their organization letterhead and sign it. Figure 2.14 shows a simple and effective sample format for you or your references to use in developing an excellent letter of recommendation.

```
            LETTER OF RECOMMENDATION
          (If possible, use company letterhead)


Date

To Whom It May Concern:
                (Or center this phrase)
            Reference Letter for Jerome Johnson

    FIRST PARAGRAPH: Mention who the letter is for, how you know
the person, and how long you have known him or her.
    SECOND PARAGRAPH: Highlight some personal character-
istics, occupational strengths, and educational background. If this infor-
mation is extensive, use two paragraphs.
    THIRD PARAGRAPH: Summarize your overall opinion of the person,
and end with a positive statement about the individual.

Signature,


    Name and Title
```

Figure 2.14. Format for Developing A Letter of Recommendation

Figure 2.15 shows an example of an actual letter of recommendation.

```
March 26, 1994


        RECOMMENDATION LETTER FOR KIM SCHLEISTER

Kim Schleister has an excellent work experience background in retail-
ing and banking. In fact, more than once she has been an award win-
ning employee gaining valuable experience in sales and management.
She also was a co-op marketing student in high school and received the
award Co-op Student of the Year.

In my classes, Kim always got involved in discussions and was willing
to assume a leadership role. Her supervising teacher for her student
teaching assignment at Dodgeville High School was also very impressed
with Kim's ability to assume responsibility. She is graduating in the top
25 students at UW-Stout.

Kim Schleister's accomplishments in business and school have been
outstanding. It is a pleasure to recommend her for a position in the
marketing field.

Sincerely,



Gary Searle, Professor
Marketing Education
```

Figure 2.15. Letter of Recommendation

TYPES OF RESUMES

Once you have developed a rough draft of all the information needed on your resume, you must decide whether a *chronological, functional,* or *combination* resume will best suit your needs.

CHRONOLOGICAL RESUMES

A **chronological resume** is more traditional and focuses on the position and employer. As the name implies, it lists education and employment history in chronological order. This type of resume works well when you have extensive work experience related to the position you are pursuing. Two different formats for preparing chronological resumes are provided in Figures 2.16 and 2.17.

FUNCTIONAL RESUMES

A **functional resume** looks much different from a chronological resume in that your skills and achievements are the focus of attention rather than the specific positions and employers you have had. The functional resume works best for individuals who are in the process of changing careers or for the first-time job seekers and people who are re-entering the job market after not working for a period of time. Two formats for preparing functional resumes are provided in Figures 2.18 and 2.19.

COMBINATION RESUMES

If you are not comfortable using a chronological or functional format, you can use a **combination resume.** As the name implies, a combination resume uses some of both formats. Some sections of your resume can be chronological and some functional—whatever format you think does the best job of selling you to the employer. Examples of combination resumes are presented in Figures 2.20 and 2.21.

Functional, chronological, and combination resumes can be organized in heading or block styles. The functional resumes in Figures 2.18 and 2.19 are formatted in the heading style. In the block style, the major categories are blocked off on the left side of the resume, as shown in Figures 2.20 and 2.21. Pick a style that you are comfortable with and that you feel gives you the most professional look.

A smart suggestion is to go to the public library, school library, or bookstore to look at the numerous resume books on the market that concentrate solely on resumes; they give multitudes of examples of each kind of resume, and tell you how to structure and organize your resume for specific positions.

GUIDELINES FOR PREPARING YOUR FINAL DRAFT RESUME

Finally, here are some guidelines to keep in mind in developing an appealing final copy of your resume.

- *Make sure your resume is professional in appearance.* Word processing is a great tool to use in constructing your resume. It gives you excellent flexibility in font styles and sizes. Use a font style that is easy on the eye; use nothing elaborate.

  Word processors enable you to use bold text to highlight categories or titles. They also give you the ability to make appropriate changes to your resume very quickly and tailor it to different positions.

  If you do not have access to a computer/word processor, you can usually find someone in the classified ads section of your local newspaper who will do this type of work for a fee. Another option is to use your public library;

```
┌─────────────────────────────────────────────────────────────────┐
│                        MARY LIM-LEE                               │
│                     1757 Barrel Lake Road                         │
│                   Winona, Minnesota 84728                         │
│                        (355) 837-2405                             │
│                                                                   │
│  CAREER GOAL:    Elementary Teaching Position.                    │
│                  Wisconsin Certification Code 42-118              │
│                                                                   │
│  EDUCATION:      University of Wisconsin-Eau Claire, Eau Claire, WI│
│                  Bachelor of Science degree in Elementary Education│
│                  Educational Psychology minor, May 1992           │
│                                                                   │
│                  University of Wisconsin-Barron County,           │
│                      Rice Lake, WI                                │
│                  Associates degree. August 1986 to May 1988       │
│                                                                   │
│  TEACHING        Woodland Elementary School, Barron, WI           │
│  EXPERIENCE:     Student Teacher, Grade 1, Spring 1992            │
│                                                                   │
│                  Cameron Elementary School, Cameron, WI           │
│                  Student Teacher, Grade 5, Spring 1992            │
│                                                                   │
│  RELEVANT        Treatment Foster Service                         │
│  EXPERIENCE:       Barron County Department of Social Services,   │
│                      Barron, WI                                   │
│                  Treatment Foster Parent. Experience in providing │
│                  therapeutic services to children who are having seri-│
│                  ous problems in their homes, schools, and communi-│
│                  ties. January 1990 to present.                   │
│                                                                   │
│  OTHER           Customer Service Representative, Farm Fleet,     │
│  EXPERIENCE:       Rice Lake, WI                                  │
│                  March 1990 to February 1991                     │
│                                                                   │
│                  Professional Model-Paris, France; Madrid Spain   │
│                  May 1989 to December 1989                        │
│                                                                   │
│                  Sporting Goods Representative, Farm Fleet,       │
│                      Rice Lake, WI                                │
│                  August 1987 to May 1989                          │
│                                                                   │
│  HONORS:         Academic Distinction (five semesters)            │
│                                                                   │
│  INTERESTS:      Photography, fishing, and hiking.                │
│                                                                   │
│  REFERENCES:     Available from: UW-Eau Claire Career Planning    │
│                      and Placement                                │
│                  Jeter Center                                     │
│                  Eau Claire, WI 54872                             │
└─────────────────────────────────────────────────────────────────┘
```

Figure 2.16. Example of a Chronological Resume

many libraries have computers that you can use. Be absolutely sure to use a letter quality printer for your resume. Printing shops are also an excellent place to
go if you want to be assured that you have a professional looking document.

- *Use good quality paper.* Go to an office supply store or print shop and buy a
  high quality bond paper. Many people use a colored paper for their resume.
  The thought behind colored paper is that it will help set your resume apart
  from the rest of the stack. While this is true, you must be conservative in what

```
                            MARY E. SCHAFFER
                              Rt. 3 Box 197
                        Wentworth, Washington 54894
                             (555) 398-7047

        EDUCATION        Maple Northwestern High School
                         Maple, Washington
                         Studies: College Prep, Marketing
                         GPA: 3.9

        WORK EXPERIENCE

        Waitress         Louis Cafe
                         Superior, Washington
                         1987 - 1989

        Sales            AVON
                         Wentworth, Washington
                         1987 - 1989

        Child Care       Patty and Jan Miller
                         Wentworth, Washington
                         1986 - 1989

                         Cindy and Steve Kurcharski
                         Wentworth, Washington
                         1986 - 1989

        ACTIVITIES       DECA (Vice President, President), FBLA (Vice
                         President), Drama, Forensics, Volleyball, Softball

        REFERENCES       Available upon request
```

Figure 2.17. Example of a Chronological Resume

colors to use. Colors such as off-white, eggshell, parchment, buckskin, slate gray, or baby blue are sometimes used. Stay away from bright colors such as yellow, red, orange, etc. Again, your print shop or office supply store can help you out with your selection. If you use colored paper, get colored envelopes to match your cover letter.

- *Be sure to proofread your resume carefully.* Improper grammar and spelling errors are serious problems that have kept people from getting the jobs they wanted. It will be a problem if you do not use a good proofreader to catch any misspellings or poor punctuation. Remember, your resume is the first impression an employer has of you, and you want it to be favorable.

- *Pick a format and style that is not flashy or gaudy.* Items such as crests and photographs of yourself are not recommended. Have a friend check your resume for appearance.

- *Choose an appropriate margin.* There is no standard rule concerning top, bottom, left, and right margins. These margins should depend on how much information you have on your resume and how you organize it. The key thing to remember is that your resume must appeal to the eye, read easily, and look uncluttered. White space sells, and it can work for you. The information should be well balanced on the page.

TONY MARKOWICZ
667 Waller Street
Montgomery, Alabama 27802
(555) 723-5541

OBJECTIVE: Construction Management Position

PROFESSIONAL EXPERIENCE

COMMERCIAL PROJECTS
St. Luke's Hospital, Atlanta; Montgomery School District 101; HUD housing projects; Atlanta City Hall.

PROJECT MANAGEMENT
* Assistant Manager for two successful construction companies.
* Worked on single family dwellings, spec houses and commercial buildings.
  Hired, trained, motivated and supervised crews of 10-20 employees.
  Responsible for completion of projects within budget and on time.
  Located qualified vendors and negotiated contracts.
  Responsible for acquiring zoning and building permits.
  Carried out effective on-site supervision, maintained safety standards.

CLIENT RELATIONS
* Liaison between contractors, engineers, architects and clients.
* Effectively negotiated cost estimation with clients.

EDUCATION
* Associate Degree in Wood Techniques; Dade County Technical College, June, 1985

EMPLOYMENT HISTORY
* Project Manager; Villeneuve Builders, Montgomery, Alabama 2/90 to present
* Construction Manager; ABC Roofing Inc., Atlanta, Georgia 11/87 - 2/90
* Carpenter; Peterson Builders, Atlanta, Georgia 6/85 - 11/87

REFERENCES
Available on request.

Figure 2.18. Example of a Functional Resume

SUMMARY

Resume is a French word that means "a short history of one's life." It is an organized outline of a job applicant's background, including work experience, education, and accomplishments. A strong resume is an extremely important component of the job search for the 1990s. The primary purpose of a resume is to provide a prospective employer with information that will influence the company to interview you.

Your resume can be used in several different ways. It can be sent, along with a cover letter, to a potential employer. The resume is also an excellent reference when you have to fill out an application form for an employer. In addition, you

DAVID GARCIA
4615 Maple Drive
Jenson Beach, Florida 42224
(555) 626-7021

PROFESSIONAL TARGET

Management level position in a national retailing/wholesaling company that emphasizes direct responsibility for project control, P&L and balance sheet project analyses and follow-through implementation of strategic goals and plans.

CAPABILITIES

- Communicating effectively in problem solving for financial and non-financial areas of a business, using practical, workable solutions for a wide range of business activities.
- Implementing at the field level corporate programs and systems to enhance the profitability of the overall business.
- Providing positive results from general concepts and goals that affect diverse aspects of a business with quantifiable P&L and balance sheet impact.

ACHIEVEMENTS

- Prepared and monitored a $1.75 million tax department budget for a Fortune 100 oil company as well as 1) streamlining projection, review and year-end allocation methods with personally designed computer programs and 2) researching/evaluating items for tax amendment purposes.
- Established and successfully managed for five years an accounting service (before its profitable divestiture) which counseled over 400 clients covering tax preparation, design of tailored accounting systems, and client representation before IRS and other government agencies.

WORK HISTORY

11/92 - present	Goldcoast Electronics, Inc. Jacksonville, FL	Controller
06/84 - 11/92	Charter Oil Company Jacksonville, FL	Tax Analyst

EDUCATION

1991	State of Florida	Certified Public
	1984	Accountant
	University of Florida	B.S., Finance

AFFILIATIONS

American Institute of Certified Public Accountants
Florida Institute of Certified Public Accountants
Data Processing Management Association

Figure 2.19. Example of a Functional Resume

should take a few extra copies to a job interview in case one of your interviewers did not receive a copy.

When writing your resume, keep in mind the following current trends in resume preparation. A resume should be limited to one page. It is proper to limit the use of personal information. Action-oriented achievements should be stressed. One or two action sentences at the beginning of the resume may replace the traditional position wanted/career objective section. Another trend is to elim-

```
                        MARIE MOONEY
                       2163 17th Avenue
                 Pittsburgh, Pennsylvania 24868
                         (555) 236-7722

CAREER OBJECTIVE      A secretarial position in which my office skills,
                      management skills, and interpersonal skills can
                      be utilized to benefit this organization.

OFFICE SKILLS AND     Typewriting: 65 wpm
OFFICE EQUIPMENT      Shorthand:   80 wpm

                      FAX Machine
                      Xerox 620 Memorywriter
                      Transcriber/Dictaphone
                      Ten-Key Adding Machine
                      Printing Calculator
                      IBM Word Processor - WordStar, WordPerfect

MANAGING SKILLS       Organized file of business ideas
                      Managed office when employers were not in
                      Managed sales staff at Francis Jewelers

INTERPERSONAL         Adaptable to different situations
SKILLS                Work well with others
                      Self-starter, do required work and more

EXPERIENCE            Nanny position (5/90 to 5/91)
                      Short Hills, New Jersey
                      Managed household, organized activities for
                      children

                      Francis Jewelers (5/86 to 2/90)
                      Pittsburgh, Pennsylvania
                      Charge of payroll, head sales clerk, controlled
                      inventory

                      Harmon Contract Glazing (2/85 to 11/85)
                      Minneapolis, MN
                      Answered telephones, directed calls, receptionist,
                      filing, typing

EDUCATION             St. Paul Technical College (1982-1984)
                      Associate of Science Degree in Secretarial
                      Science

REFERENCES            Available upon request
```

Figure 2.20. Example of a Combination Resume

inate entirely any reference to career choices or goals. Finally, video resumes are now an acceptable means of selling yourself to prospective employers.

Developing an outstanding, hard–hitting resume takes a great deal of time and effort on your part. You need to collect a variety of information for each of the categories on your resume. The following categories are typical on most resumes: personal information; position wanted; or career objective; education; work experience; activities, interests, and awards; and references.

```
                        BLIA K. VANG
                        1167 Freeland
                     Freeport, Maine 54723
                       (555) 458-2759

OBJECTIVE:     Marketing and Management

SUMMARY:       Experience in management, marketing, sales, super-
               vision, and public relations. Familiar with filing and
               typing, correspondence, switchboard operations, word
               processing, maintaining inventory, payroll,
               opening/closing operations, and visual displays.

EXPERIENCE:    Visual Merchandiser    8/91 - Present
               Fashion Bug and Fashion Bug Plus, Freeport, Maine
               Duties included: Customer/employee supervision,
               computer show reports, payroll, opening/closing
               operations, and ticket and concession sales.

               Associate Manager    2/89 - 7/91
               Excellence Cinema 3 Theater, Freeport Maine
               Duties included: Customer/employee supervision,
               computer show reports, payroll, opening/closing
               operations, and ticket and concession sales.

               Sales/Receiving/Sales Associate    6/90 - 8/91
               Wal Mart, Freeport, Maine
               Duties included: Customer service, maintaining
               inventory, sales and receiving, and weekly orders.

               Clerical Assistant    8/89 - 5/90
               Central Maine Technical College Freeport, Maine,
               Duties included:   Typing, filing, correspondence,
               and switchboard operaitons.

EDUCATION:     8/88 - 5/90  Central Main Technical College
               Freeport, Maine, two-year Associate Degree in
               Marketing

               8/84 - 5/88   Luck Public High School, Luck, Maine
               Business and general courses studied.

PERSONAL       Volunteer, downhill skiing, cross-country skiing,
INTERESTS:     water-skiing, snowmobiling, sewing, stock car racing.

PERSONAL       Furnished on request.
REFERENCES:
```

Figure 2.21. Example of a Combination Resume

The three standard types of resumes are chronological, functional, and combination resumes. The chronological resume lists education and employment history by dates in a past-to-present order. The functional resume looks much different, in that your skills and achievements are the focus of attention. The combination resume uses some of both formats.

Your resume must present a professional appearance. It should be prepared using a word processor on a high quality, conservative bond paper. Use a good proofreader. Pick a format and style that are not flashy or gaudy, and provide reader eye appeal. Choose top, bottom, right, and left margins that work for the amount of information you have on your resume. Paying attention to these kinds of details will enhance your chances for successful job searching.

QUESTIONS FOR REVIEW AND DISCUSSION

1. What is a resume? What are the other names for a resume?

_____

_____

_____

_____

_____

2. What is the primary purpose of a resume? What are the different uses for a resume?

_____

_____

_____

_____

_____

3. Why is a resume a critical tool in your search for a job?

_____

_____

_____

_____

_____

4. What are the resume trends for the 1990s?

_____

_____

_____

_____

_____

5. What kinds of personal information should you list on your resume?

_____

_____

_____

_____

_____

6. Is it acceptable to list more than one position wanted on your resume?

_____

_____

_____

_____

_____

7. Is the heart of your resume the educational section or the work experience section? Why?

_____

_____

_____

_____

_____

8. What is the proper way to list work experience on your resume?

_____

_____

_____

_____

9. Why would a prospective employer be interested in knowing your activities, interests, and hobbies?

_____

_____

_____

_____

10. What are the differences between a chronological and functional resume?

_____

_____

_____

_____

11. What are five guidelines to consider in preparing the final draft of your resume?

_____

_____

_____

_____

_____

CASE STUDY

Critique the Safy Khaled resume in Figure 2.22. Is it a chronological, functional, or combination resume? Identify as many things wrong with it as you can.

_____

_____

SAFY KHALED

Permanent address
1002 Ingalls Rd.
St. Louis, MO 67901
555-235-0872

PROFESSIONAL OBJECTIVE   To obtain a position in Marketing

WORK EXPERIENCE	POSITION AND DUTIES	DATES
United States Army	Classified mail courier, recruiter	1/73 - 9/74
University of Missouri Recreation Center Columbia, MO 68701	Recreation Center Attendant	8/77 - 5/78
Nabors Drug Store 1978 St. Louis, MO 26147	Salesman-Worked under a trainer program that involved all aspects of the store	Summer
Garret Freightlines Present St. Paul, MN 55109	Freight unloader and merchandise checker	8/78 -

EDUCATION	MAJOR
Southwest Wisconsin Vocational Technical Institute, Fennimore, WI	Business Finance - one year of courses in Business & Finance
University of Missouri Columbia, MO 68701 GRADUATION GPA.: 3.1	B.S. in Marketing 12/16/78 Minor: Business Concentration: Retailing and Marketing

ORGANIZATIONS AND ACTIVITIES
   Distributive Education Clubs of America 2,3,4 Columbia Jaycees 2,3,4

AWARDS AND OFFICES
   Chancellor's Academic Award one semester, Vice President,
   U of M DECA 77,
   Chapter Director Columbia Jaycees 77.

Birthplace: Edgewood, IA   Height: 5′10″   Health: Excellent
Birthdate: 11/9/52   Weight: 200 lbs.   Marital status: Married

Further credentials and references will be furnished upon request.

Figure 2.22. Safy Khaled's Resume

PROJECT

Type a new resume for Mr. Kahled using the concepts and skills learned in this chapter. Exchange resumes with a class partner and compare your corrections. Submit your final copy to your instructor for additional evaluation.

The Cover Letter

OBJECTIVES

After completing this chapter, you should be able to:

1. Explain the purpose of a cover letter.

2. Give examples of appropriate times to use a cover letter.

3. Prepare a dynamic cover letter.

4. Discuss the use of a letter of inquiry.

5. Use general letter writing guidelines.

6. Identify specific cover letter guidelines.

THE COVER LETTER CONSIDERED

An important component of the job-seeking process is the formal written communication called a **cover letter**. This business letter is sent with the resume to an employer, requesting consideration for a specific position with the organization. When the cover letter and resume are actually inserted into an envelope, the cover letter is on top so the employer will read it first. The letter "covers" the resume in this process and earned its name from that sequence.

Some job seekers simply send their resume to employers without a cover letter. This practice is not advisable unless you have such an outstanding background that your resume alone will inspire an employer to bring you in for an interview. In today's job market, there are dozens and often hundreds of qualified people applying for the same position. The cover letter gives you one more opportunity to display your job seeking knowledge and skill. It allows you to develop some personal rapport with the employer and highlight your interest in a specific position.

THE PURPOSE OF A COVER LETTER

The importance of a cover letter becomes clearer when the applicant understands the purpose of this communication. Certainly, the major purpose must be to stimulate the employer to read your resume. Many employers simply scan your cover letter and resume, and then make a decision about reading the details. The cover letter is going to make that all-important first impression. The cover letter also allows you to mention the specific position that interests you, highlight your background, and request an interview. The overall goal of sending the cover letter and resume is to obtain a job interview.

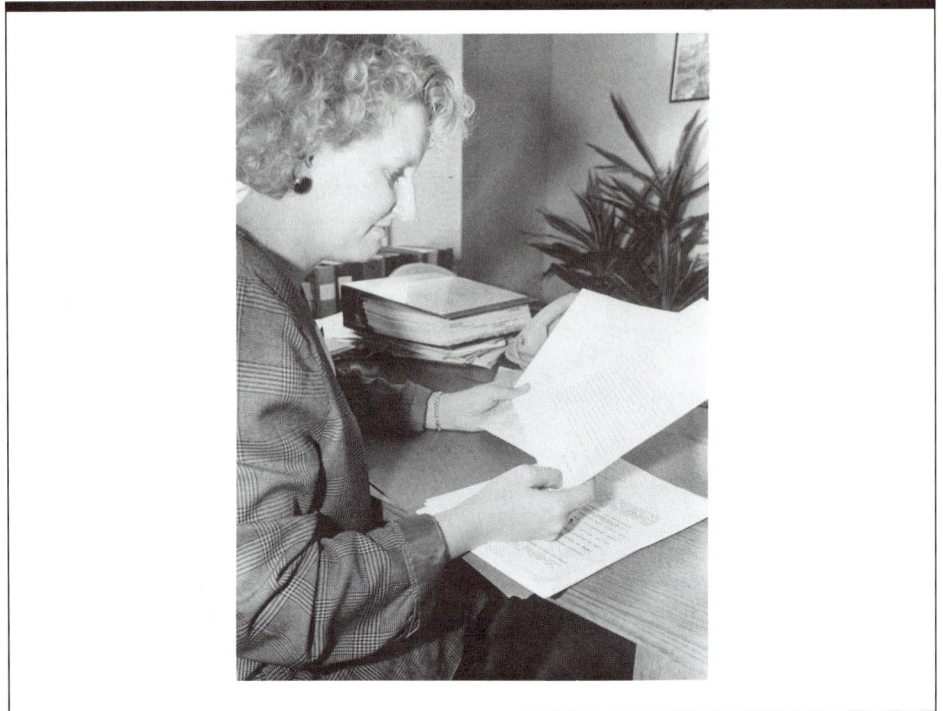

Your cover letter is the first thing a prospective employer will see and read when reviewing your resume, so the more impressive it makes you look, the better your chances for that all-important first interview. (Photo by Mary Langenfeld.)

MAKING YOUR FIRST IMPRESSION

Job seekers often spend a great amount of time planning, organizing, and developing their resumes, but make the mistake of spending far less time working on their cover letters. The cover letter represents your first written impression with an employer, and it can be a key element in your job search. It is a real challenge to prepare an effective, hard-hitting cover letter that brings a successful response.

The example in Figure 3.1 is a cover letter used by a university teacher who is applying for a similar position at another school. Since the letter is well written and follows sound principles of written communication, it could be changed and adapted to fit positions in most any field.

USING YOUR COVER LETTER

The cover letter and resume work together to assist you in getting a job interview. One should not be used without the other.

The question, then, is "What circumstances dictate the use of a cover letter?" The answer is found in the idea that the cover letter always mentions your interest in a specific position. You may hear about these openings through advertisements and personal contacts or you may decide to use a cold canvass approach.

ADVERTISEMENTS

Advertisements refer to what are commonly called *classified* or *want ads* in publications like your local newspaper. If you are willing to relocate, be sure to check

```
250 McClelland Drive
Eau Claire, Wisconsin 54703
May 9, 1994


Three Lakes University
Personnel Department
3301 Orange Avenue
Fort Lauderdale, Florida 33314

Dear Educator:

Recently, I saw your vacancy announcement for a Chairperson in the
Chronicle.  Please consider the enclosed resume as my application for
this interesting administrative position.  Presently, I am Chair of the
Communications, Education and Training Department at a regional
university in the Wisconsin system.  The opportunity to obtain a posi-
tion at Three Lakes University, and return to the South, is very ap-
pealing to my husband and me.

Your position announcement stated several qualifications that have
been integral components of my present and past experiences.  I have
successfully held teaching and administrative positions at the sec-
ondary and collegiate levels, taught evening adult classes at the
junior college level, and have been a state department of education
supervisor.

These are certainly exciting and challenging times for education.  I
have been involved in a wide range of education activities at the local,
state, national and international levels.  Our marketing teacher educa-
tion program has 129 undergraduate students, the largest in the
United States, and we were just selected as the Outstanding Chapter
of the Year at the national marketing conference in Denver.

I am eager to learn more about your position at Three Lakes
University.  Please feel free to contact me at home (555-237-6985) or
office (555-237-5483).  I will anxiously await your reply.

Sincerely,

Yolanda B. Angelou

Yolanda B. Angelou
Professor, Marketing Education
```

Figure 3-1. A Model Cover Letter

newspapers like *The New York Times, Dallas Morning News, Los Angeles Times*, and *The Wall Street Journal*, as well as any trade journals that are popular in your field of interest. Want ads are the most obvious and common means of finding job openings. Once you find an advertisement that interests you, tailor your cover letter to the specific position, include your resume, and send these credentials to the employer.

PERSONAL CONTACTS

There is a good deal of truth to the old saying, "It's not what you know, but who you know." Personal contacts are excellent sources for job leads. A women's sportswear buyer told the marketing representatives who called on him that he was interested in a new and exciting challenge. Within two weeks, one of

THE COVER LETTER

Mary Kohls-Kuntz

As vice-president and treasurer for General Tele-Communications, Inc. in Northbrook, Illinois, Mary Kohls-Kuntz is involved in the company's hiring process. In one day alone, she reviewed twenty-six resumes and cover letters for an available position in her firm's accounts payable department. Ms. Kohls agreed to explain what she looks for when reading a cover letter from a job applicant.

Mary Kohls likes to see a familiar name that can be used for checking references. Networking works with her. If you happen to have been recommended to a company by a specific person, she suggests you mention his or her name in your first paragraph.

How you portray yourself is also important. If you have done your homework and researched the company to which you are applying for a job, make sure you make the employers aware of this by mentioning how your background fits in with their needs.

If previous employers, teachers or friends have made you aware that you possess some outstanding characteristics, be sure that you work these into your cover letter. At General Tele-Communications, Ms. Kohls likes to see these characteristics listed and highlighted in the applicant's second paragraph. If you can list such characteristics on a separate line or two, you will draw the employer's attention to them and give your chances for an interview a boost.

Mary Kohls also looks for the mention of a specific salary in the cover letters that she reads. If a salary is mentioned, she immediately begins to make a judgement as to whether such a salary fits in with her company's pay scale. Unless expressly asked to state a salary requirement, you will do best to avoid discussing this issue until you are in an interview situation.

For busy individuals such as Ms. Kohls, wordiness in cover letters is a major concern. Letters that use long, fancy words to impress and take two sentences to say what could be said in one are frowned upon. Take a lesson from the person who sent in a three-page cover letter to precede a three-page resume: this individual's efforts went straight to the waste can for recycling.

An employer wants to know that an applicant is interested in a particular job, so if your cover letter looks "canned," Ms. Kohls recommends that you change your approach. Make the employer feel that you want to work for *them*.

A clean cover letter is also important to the individuals who have to read and evaluate it. Letters with spots, smudges, and visible correction fluid make a poor first impression. To Ms. Kohl's way of thinking, sloppy cover letters come from sloppy people with low personal standards. Do you expect that such people ever reach the interview stage with General Tele-Communications?

A very important aspect of an individual's cover letter is the stated, or unstated, career goals. If you want an employer to believe you are interested in working for *them*, Ms. Kohls suggests that you make sure you mention how the job you are seeking and the company you are seeking it with fit into your short- and long-range career aspirations.

Finally, when reading cover letters, Mary Kohls looks for mention of the applicants' present work status. Are they employed or out of work? If an applicant is unemployed, Ms. Kohls wants to know if there was a problem with the last employer. She says that over half the people applying with her company have been terminated from their last employer, most of them victims of downsizing or restructuring in the 1990s rather than terminated for poor performance. If this is the case with you, she recommends that you face it head on and mention it in your cover letter.

the reps told him she knew of a buyer's position that would be available soon. The buyer tailored his cover letter to suit the specific position and used the marketing rep as a referral in the letter. He got the new job. This anecdote is a good example of effective utilization of a cover letter.

COLD CANVASS

Successful job seekers often take the initiative and do a cold canvass search for employment. **Cold canvass** means you do not have prior knowledge of any job openings, so you canvass employers by sending out a cover letter and resume, with the hope that someone can use your talents and experience. Cold canvass is more effective when seeking technically oriented jobs and less effective when seeking management positions.

The cold canvass is most effective when you know specifically what kind of positions may be available, and when you have a certain local or regional geographical area that interests you. For example, hospitals have physical therapists who may help you find hospital mailing lists. Your cold canvass cover letter and resume might focus on physical therapy positions, and you could canvass on a regional, state, or national basis. This process is an excellent use of your specifically designed cover letter.

THE PREPARATION OF COVER LETTERS

There isn't any one perfect or absolutely correct way to write a cover letter, but there are many helpful guidelines to consider. The information you include in your letter will depend on your specific background and the job you are seeking. You should have a good idea of the job description when you write a cover letter, so the task is to sell your qualifications for the specific position. The successful cover letter will blend your qualifications into the job description and establish the benefit of hiring you to the employer.

Before you write your cover letter, a good first step is to make a list of your personal assets. For example, a secretary could list the different types of software used on the daily job. This list might include office machine skills, meetings planning experience, financial reports data, product or service knowledge, or anything else specific to past experience as a secretary.

A well-thought-out list can then be used to highlight whichever qualifications and accomplishments you need to take from the list to develop an individualized, job-specific cover letter. Emphasize the qualities that will interest an employer. Think about what you would like to read if you were hiring a person for your company. It is a good idea to try and understand the employer's viewpoint throughout the entire job-seeking process.

Each cover letter must be your best work; it establishes a professional first impression. Word-processing equipment, including a letter quality printer, presents an excellent image. Use of a computer also allows easy changes to a letter so that it can be used with changes for future cover letters, especially if you use the cold canvass approach. Often only the address, and possibly the first paragraph, of your letter will require changes. Computer equipment is available for rent, or you may wish to use a professional printing service. Be sure to establish a price before you accept such services.

To establish a professional image and make a favorable first impression, your cover letter must also use perfect grammar, punctuation, and spelling. In other words, your use of the English language must bring your letter to the top of the employer's list of applicants. Be as concise as you can while still selling your qualifications and accomplishments. A cover letter should never, ever exceed one page. Employers simply will not take the time to read a two- or three-page cover letter.

Employers like people with a good positive attitude and those who project confidence. You can create this impression by requesting an interview at the employer's convenience or even by suggesting a time when you will be available. You can say you will call after the employer receives your letter, to confirm a time for an interview. You can also project confidence in the language of your cover letter. Use words like *teamwork, success, initiative*, and *contribution*. Employers do not want to hire persons who consider themselves failures.

Figure 3.1 offered an example of a well-written, four-paragraph cover letter. It is also very common to use a three-paragraph cover letter for many positions. Following are descriptions and examples of each paragraph in a three-paragraph cover letter format.

THE INTRODUCTORY PARAGRAPH

The first paragraph of your cover letter should explain why you are writing the letter. Mention the specific job or type of work that interests you, and describe how you found out about the opening with the organization. Figure 3.2 follows these guidelines and is still brief and to the point.

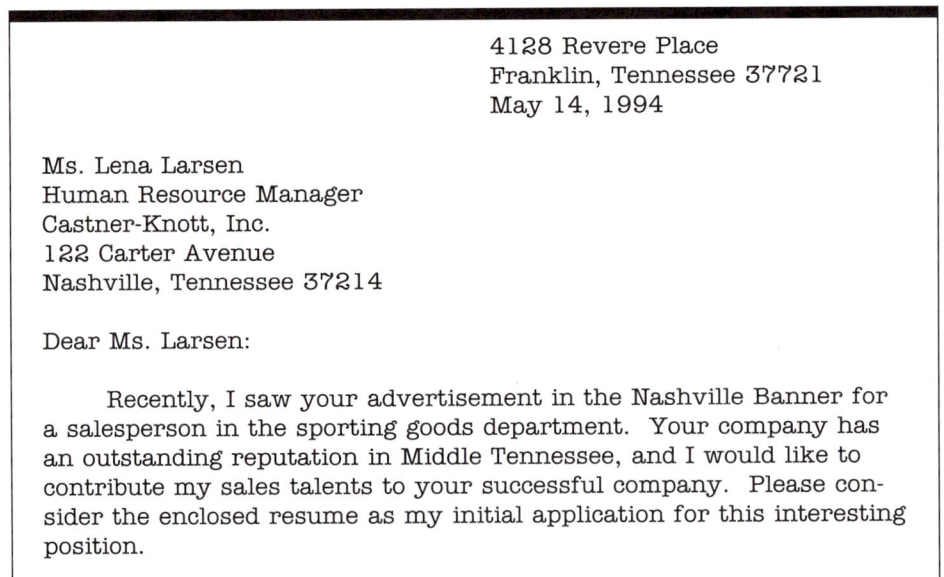

```
                                        4128 Revere Place
                                        Franklin, Tennessee 37721
                                        May 14, 1994


Ms. Lena Larsen
Human Resource Manager
Castner-Knott, Inc.
122 Carter Avenue
Nashville, Tennessee 37214

Dear Ms. Larsen:

     Recently, I saw your advertisement in the Nashville Banner for
a salesperson in the sporting goods department.  Your company has
an outstanding reputation in Middle Tennessee, and I would like to
contribute my sales talents to your successful company.  Please con-
sider the enclosed resume as my initial application for this interesting
position.
```

Figure 3-2. The Introductory Paragraph of a Cover Letter

Note how the key words *reputation, contribute, sales talents*, and *successful company* are used to enhance the introductory paragraph.

THE BODY OF THE LETTER

The second paragraph of your cover letter should explain to the employer why you are interested in this specific position. Mention your potential contributions; highlight academic background, previous work experience, and specific achievements if they apply to the vacant position. Figure 3.3 offers an example of a good second paragraph, for the sporting goods sales position at Castner-Knott, Inc.

> Sports is a very important part of my life. I am co-captain of a neighborhood softball team and played three years of basketball in high school where I was the leading scorer my senior year. Bowling and hunting are my favorite recreation sports. These sporting activities should help me meet the qualifications for your sales position and allow me to contribute my sporting knowledge to the continued success of Caster-Knott, Inc.

Figure 3-3. The Body of a Cover Letter

The applicant has explained her interest in this position and blended her sports background into the qualifications for the job, even though she has no previous sales experience in sporting goods. The paragraph expresses confidence and success.

THE CLOSING PARAGRAPH

The last paragraph of your cover letter should request an interview. Mention when and where you can be contacted, or when you will be in the employer's area, if that is appropriate. End the closing paragraph with a positive statement or question. Figure 3.4 is an excellent example, showing the last paragraph for the sporting goods sales position.

> Please allow me to explain my strong interest and qualifications in your sporting goods sales position through a personal interview. You may contact me on weekdays between 8:00 AM and 4:30 PM at 555-746-5481, or at home 555-746-2981. I will anxiously await your reply.
>
> Sincerely,
>
> *Mary Ann Bracey*
>
> MARY ANN BRACEY
>
> Enclosure

Figure 3-4. The Closing Paragraph of a Cover Letter

The applicant has closed the cover letter in a decisive way that again projects confidence. She has emphasized her desire to explain her qualifications more completely in a personal interview. Figure 3.5 shows the completed three-paragraph cover letter.

The three-paragraph cover letter is appropriate for this applicant's experience. If you have a wide range of qualifications and achievements, you could insert another paragraph, as shown in Figure 3.1. In that example, the applicant simply added another paragraph to the body of the letter and emphasized additional facts and details. Another excellent four-paragraph cover letter is shown in Figure 3.6.

4128 Revere Place
Franklin, Tennessee 37215
May 14, 1994

Ms. Lena Larsen
Human Resource Manager
Castner-Knott, Inc.
122 Carter Avenue
Nashville, Tennessee 37214

Dear Ms. Larsen:

Recently, I saw your advertisement in the Nashville Banner for a salesperson in the sporting goods department. Your company has an outstanding reputation in Middle Tennessee, and I would like to contribute my sales talents to your successful company. Please consider the enclosed resume as my initial application for this interesting position.

Sports are a very important part of my life. I am co-captain of a neighborhood softball team and played three years of basketball in high school where I was the leading scorer my senior year. Bowling and hunting are my favorite recreation sports. These sporting activities should help me meet the qualifications for your sales position and allow me to contribute my sporting knowledge to the continued success of Caster-Knott, Inc.

Please allow me to explain my strong interest and qualifications in your sporting goods sales position through a personal interview. You may contact me on weekdays between 8:00 AM and 4:30 PM at 555-746-5481, or at home 555-746-2981. I will anxiously await your reply.

Sincerely,

Mary Ann Bracey

MARY ANN BRACEY

Enclosure

Figure 3-5. A Three Paragraph Cover Letter

1595 Harmony Street
Portland, Oregon 90125
January 10, 1994

Mr. George Vitali
Shop Manager
Vitali Bros. Auto Shop
Route 5, Box 1192
Eureka, California 91875

Dear Mr. Vitali:

My friend, Sid Rosen, knows your brother, and he recently told Arnold about your need for another body and fender repair person. Please consider me an applicant for this job.

As you can see from the enclosed resume, I studied body and fender repair for two years at Central Technical College and received an associate degree. I made excellent grades in my classes, learned a great deal about the business, and was treasurer of our automobile repair student organization.

For the last two years, I have worked part-time at Maxine's Auto Repair here in Roseburg. The two years of practical experience should prepare me for your job, and allow me to contribute to the successful operation of your shop. I think it would be very exciting to live and work in beautiful northern California.

Please let me know when I can come down for an interview. I can be contacted after 6:00 p.m. at (555) 832-1493. I will anxiously await your reply.

Sincerely,

Lynne Scherlin-Rockman

Lynne Scherlin-Rockman

Enclosure

Figure 3-6. The Four-Paragraph Cover Letter

THE LETTER OF INQUIRY

Another type of application letter is called the letter of inquiry. It is used to inquire about the possibility of a job opening when you do not know if any vacancy exists. Since you are unsure of any openings, the letter of inquiry is written in more general terms to cover more potential possibilities.

Experts disagree on whether to include a resume with a letter of inquiry. Some say it is a waste of time and effort, because you will only get a very low response from employers when you send this type of letter. Others say the resume details more of your qualifications, and therefore increases your chances of an employer response. Including a resume, even though you are not applying for a specific open position, certainly will not hinder your chances for a response. It may well be worth the effort. Figure 3.7 shows a well–written letter of inquiry.

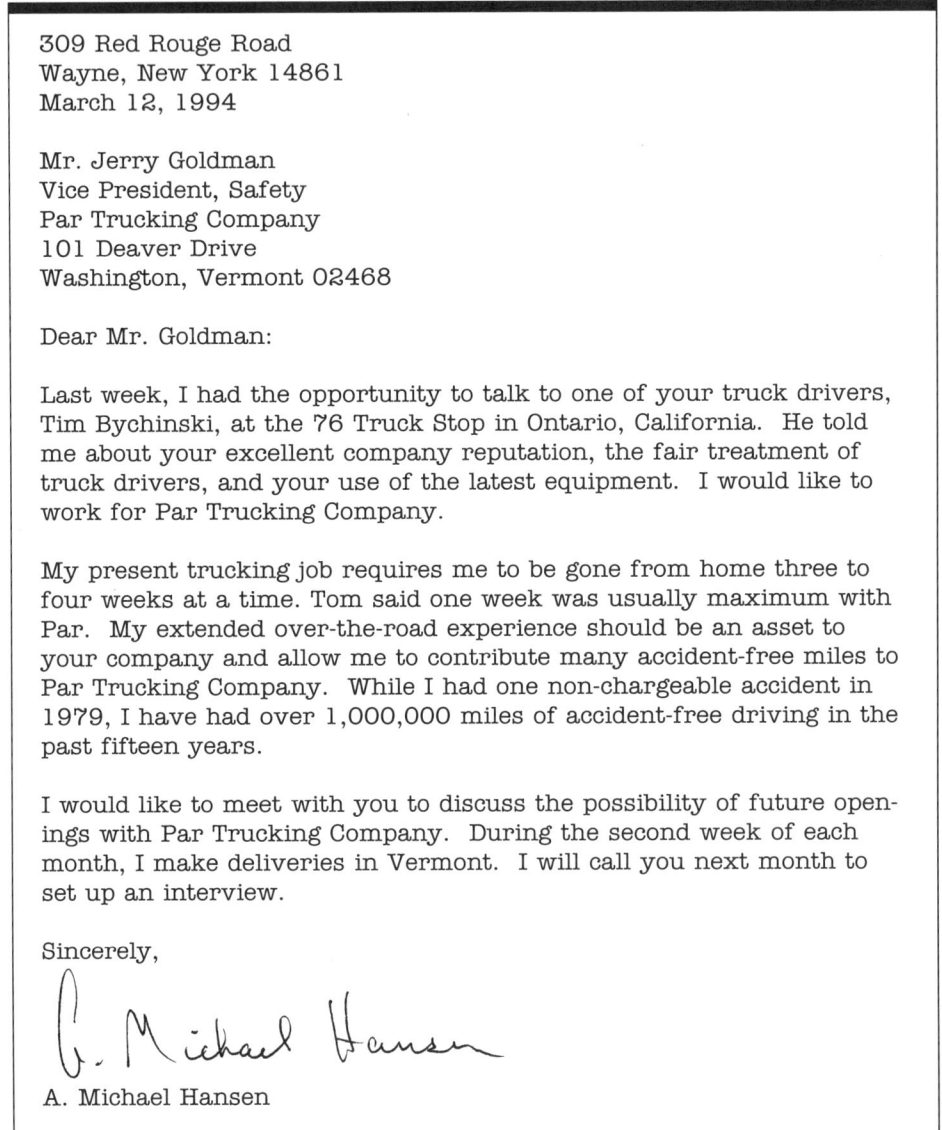

---

309 Red Rouge Road
Wayne, New York 14861
March 12, 1994

Mr. Jerry Goldman
Vice President, Safety
Par Trucking Company
101 Deaver Drive
Washington, Vermont 02468

Dear Mr. Goldman:

Last week, I had the opportunity to talk to one of your truck drivers, Tim Bychinski, at the 76 Truck Stop in Ontario, California. He told me about your excellent company reputation, the fair treatment of truck drivers, and your use of the latest equipment. I would like to work for Par Trucking Company.

My present trucking job requires me to be gone from home three to four weeks at a time. Tom said one week was usually maximum with Par. My extended over-the-road experience should be an asset to your company and allow me to contribute many accident-free miles to Par Trucking Company. While I had one non-chargeable accident in 1979, I have had over 1,000,000 miles of accident-free driving in the past fifteen years.

I would like to meet with you to discuss the possibility of future openings with Par Trucking Company. During the second week of each month, I make deliveries in Vermont. I will call you next month to set up an interview.

Sincerely,

A. Michael Hansen

Figure 3-7. The Letter of Inquiry

Mr. Hansen's letter of inquiry follows the same guidelines as the previous cover letters. He develops another personal characteristic—honesty—when he mentions a past accident. The safe number of miles he has driven and his years of employment would be an asset to any trucking company, and Mr. Goldman will surely be waiting for his telephone call. Note also that a resume was not included in this letter of inquiry, but it easily could have been if Mr. Hansen felt it would help his chance for employment. He may not wish to include the resume, since he has an excellent letter of inquiry that represents fifteen years of successful employment.

GENERAL LETTER WRITING GUIDELINES

In your job-seeking process, you may choose to use the cover letter or letter of inquiry. In either case, there are some general letter-writing guidelines that should always be followed.

Figure 3.1 is an example of a block style letter format. Notice that each line starts evenly on the left hand margin. Figure 3.5 uses the indented format for the return address, paragraphs, and complementary close. Either style is acceptable, so you should base your choice on which format has the most eye appeal to you. Try both styles for your letter, and then choose the one you think will look most appealing to an employer. You may want a second opinion on appeal. It is always a good idea.

Letter-writing guidelines in textbooks will tell you how many lines to use for spacing in a business letter. For example, the first paragraph of the letter should start two lines below the salutation (an example of a salutation is "Dear Ms. Jones"). Also, always use a one-inch left margin. But your letter may be shorter or longer, and therefore not appropriate for these guidelines. The best procedure is to use a computer word-processing program and experiment with your letter format until it meets the eye-appeal test. This advice comes from an experienced professional secretary.

The following points are important to remember in the preparation of all business letters:

1. Use consistent margin settings, either indented or block style, as shown in Figures 3.1 and 3.5.

2. Correctly place your address on the letter. Note the variations in Figures 3.5 and 3.6.

3. Know where to properly place the company address.

4. Use the correction salutation. (Dear Mrs., Ms., or Mr. White.)

5. Know the proper closing for your letter. You cannot go wrong with "Sincerely." Avoid trite closings like "Yours Truly" or "Very Truly Yours."

6. Always sign your name.

7. All letters should be typed and stored on a computer disc to facilitate easy alterations for future use.

8. Use a high quality computer printer.

9. Neatness is absolutely necessary.

10. White, high quality 8 1/2" x 11" bond paper is always correct; however, some "experts" suggest appropriate soft colors like grey and beige.

11. Only one side of the paper should be used.

12. Spelling and grammar must be checked and double-checked. Computer spell check programs can miss some errors.

13. Use a good proofreader to ensure correctness.

An experienced typist can help you with the above principles, or you may refer to a business letter writing textbook in the library.

SPECIFIC COVER APPLICATION LETTER GUIDELINES

Following are some important ideas that relate specifically to application letters:

1. Whenever possible, address your letter to a particular person in the organization. If you cannot determine the person's name, use a title like "Dear Department Manager" or "Human Resource Coordinator." Avoid "Dear Sir or Madam" if you do not know which is correct.

2. Make a personal inventory of your assets, and shape the application letter to emphasize them.

3. Highlight what you can do for the employer rather than what the employer can do for you.

4. Be positive, and express confidence by using words like *contribution, success, teamwork,* and *initiative.*

5. Avoid the common mistake of beginning too many sentences with the pronoun "I," and don't begin more than one paragraph with "I."

6. Always request an interview and indicate your availability, if appropriate.

7. Note any enclosures you send in your letter.

8. Avoid the use of abbreviations like St., Dr., and Calif. this practice will help you develop consistency in your application letter.

9. Lastly, always use the "you" attitude throughout your application letter.

These ideas will help ensure your opportunity to be considered for an interview. Many employers receive hundreds of application letters for job openings, and they set high initial standards for job candidates. Your first impression application letter must exceed those standards of excellence.

SUMMARY

An important component of the job-seeking process is the formal written communication called a cover letter. It is sent, along with a resume, to request an interview for a specific vacant position with an organization. Some job seekers simply send their resume without a cover letter, but this practice is not recommended unless you have an exceptionally strong background of qualifications for the position. The major purpose of a cover letter is to stimulate the employer's interest in you so that you can obtain a job interview.

Job seekers need to devote as much quality time to the development of a cover letter as they do to the design of their resume. The cover letter represents your first written impression with an employer, and it can be a key element in a successful job search.

The cover letter and resume will work together to help you get a job interview. They are used together when you know of a specific opening with an organization. The three most common ways to find openings are through newspaper advertisements, personal contacts, and the cold canvass approach.

There is no one perfect way to write a cover letter, but there are guidelines to consider. The successful cover letter will blend your qualifications into the vacant position's job description and establish to the employer the benefits of hiring you. It is a good idea to make a list of your qualifications and achievements before you write the cover letter. Then you can emphasize the qualities that will interest an employer. Read your letter from the employer's viewpoint and ask yourself: Do I want to interview this applicant? Each cover letter must be your best work in order to establish a quality professional image. Your letter should project confidence and a positive attitude.

Most cover letters consist of three paragraphs. The introductory paragraph should explain your purpose for writing, mention the job you are seeking, and describe how you found out about the opening. The second paragraph should describe your interest in the position, mention your potential contribution to the organization, and highlight your background. You may wish to insert an additional paragraph if you have a wide range of qualifications and achievements. The last paragraph of your cover letter should request an interview, mention when and where you can be contacted, and end with a positive statement or question.

Another type of cover letter is called the letter of inquiry. It is used to inquire about the possibility of a job opening when you do not know if any vacancy exists. It is especially good to use for a cold canvass of companies to determine present or future openings.

You may choose to use a cover letter or letter of inquiry based on your specific circumstances. Regardless of which approach you use, you must follow good general business letter writing guidelines as well as guidelines specific to application letters.

QUESTIONS FOR REVIEW AND DISCUSSION

1. What are cover letters and letters of inquiry? Describe the major difference between these two letters of application.

   _____

   _____

   _____

2. Is it advisable to send your resume to an employer without including a cover letter? Explain your answer.

   _____

   _____

   _____

3. What circumstances dictate the use of a cover letter? A letter of inquiry?

   _____

   _____

   _____

4. When is a cold canvass most effective in a job search?

   _____

   _____

   _____

5. What first step should be completed before you write a cover letter?

_____

_____

6. What are five ways to develop your professional image in a cover letter?

_____

_____

7. Is it better to use a three- or a four-paragraph cover letter? Explain your answer.

_____

_____

8. What are three things that would be found in each paragraph of a three-paragraph cover letter?

_____

_____

_____

9. What are four general business letter writing guidelines?

_____

_____

_____

10. What are four specific cover letter guidelines?

_____

_____

_____

CASE STUDY

Figure 3.8 is a sample of a poorly written cover letter. Evaluate the letter and see how many errors you can correct. Your instructor may want you to rewrite the letter and use the guidelines found in this chapter.

324 Colfax Rd.
Elk Mound, NJ 54701
Jan. 2, 1994

Ms. Kim Maloney
Director
Michaels Variey Store
24 W. 12th St.
Nolensville, NJ 01324

Dear Ms. Linda Ludwikoski:

I am applying for a cashier's job. I saw your ad in the paper about two weeks ago.

I have never been a cashier before, but I can sure learn fast. I have taken business math in high school and I was really food at it. My resume is attached.

I know a girl who works for another store and she said she would show me how to use their cash register late some nite. this and my business math should qualify me for your job.

I will come in friday at 2:00PM for an interview. If you can't make it, forget it. I'll come again next Friday. I really want this job bad, because my best friend lives in Nolensville.

Yours Truly,

May B. Wright

May B. Wright

Attachment

Figure 3-8. Cover Letter

PROJECT

In the following space, write an outstanding cover letter based on the information in this chapter. Make up the situation to fit your own desire for a job. You may respond to a newspaper advertisement of your choice. Your instructor may wish to have you type your letter after you fill in the spaces below. This activity will provide valuable experience in developing your personal cover letter. Use the modified block style of letter writing.

_____

_____

_____

_____

_____

_____

_____

_____

_____

_____

_____

_____

_____

_____

_____

_____

_____

_____

_____

_____

In the space below, write an outstanding letter of inquiry based on the information in this chapter. Select a state other than your own and write your letter to an organization of your own interest to see if a position may be available now or in the future. Be creative in your approach to this project. Use the block style of letter writing.

_____

_____

_____

_____

_____

_____

_____

_____

_____

_____

_____

_____

_____

_____

_____

_____

_____

The Job Application Form

OBJECTIVES

After completing this chapter, you should be able to:

1. Explain why the application form is an important part of the job application process.

2. Identify what information is asked for on various job application forms.

3. Develop a personal file with information that will be needed on an application form.

4. Fill out a job application appropriately and completely, using good penmanship.

THE IMPORTANCE OF THE JOB APPLICATION FORM

The completion of a job application form is usually a requirement of all companies and businesses before they will even consider a candidate for a job interview. Next to the resume, the job application form is the employer's best opportunity to check credentials to determine whether you are a potential candidate for employment. Once your credentials are confirmed, this form will be referred to once again by the employer in your job interview.

The application form is also important to you and the employer because he or she will be judging you on the following:

- Accuracy of your data
- Spelling and grammatical ability
- Education and work experience
- Military record
- Other data relative to the job

Being both thorough and neat in filling out your job application form will ensure that you make a good impression with a prospective employer right from the start. (Photo by Mary Langenfeld.)

It may surprise you to learn that two of the most important criteria by which you may be judged are neatness and handwriting. To make a good impression, make sure you do the following:

1. Print or write as neatly as you can.

2. Use an erasable pen in case you make an error.

3. If you have time, type the information.

4. Be careful of the NAME line. Make sure to note whether the form asks for the first name last or last name first.

5. Your hands should be clean so that there are no smudges or fingerprints on your application.

Refer to the sample application forms throughout the chapter—such as the Application for Employment form in Figure 4.1—to gain an understanding of what information you will need to include on your forms. Develop a job application folder to keep track of all the data necessary to fill out an application form.

SECTIONS OF THE JOB APPLICATION FORM

Once you become familiar with the different sections of a job application form, there will be less chance that you will make a mistake in filling one out. As we progress through the topics in this chapter, jot down notes on what information you need to gather to complete an application form. The sections of the form used by most employers include:

• Personal data section

• General section

• Skills and abilities section

APPLICATION FOR EMPLOYMENT   DATE _____

PLEASE PRINT

PERSONAL

Name (first, middle, last)	Are you under 18? Yes ___ No ___ If yes, date of birth
Street Address City State Zip	Social Security Number
Telephone Number ( )	Telephone numbers where we can reach you during the day	Where did you learn of the Hospital? (Be specific)

Are you a citizen of the U.S. or legally authorized to work in the U.S.?   Yes ___   No ___

Is your spouse presently employed in a supervisory capacity at the Hospital?   Yes ___   No ___   If yes, in which department?

Have you ever worked for the Hospital? Yes ___ No ___ If yes, when Name then (if different)	Have you ever performed volunteer services for this Hospital? Yes ___ No ___ If yes, when Name then (if different)

Are you professionally licensed or registered with any professional group, association, or society?   Yes ___   No ___

Name of group _____   Registration or license number _____   State _____   Date of Expiration _____

Are you on layoff, subject to recall?   Yes ___   No ___

Read the job description for the position(s) for which you are applying. Are you in any way limited in your ability to safely carry out the assignments of the position(s) for which you are applying? ___ Yes ___ No
If yes, what would enable you to safely perform the job?

Have you ever been convicted of a crime or are any criminal charges pending against you?   Yes ___   No ___
If yes, describe in full, including date(s):

In the past three years, have you ever knowingly used any narcotics, amphetamines or barbiturates, other than those prescribed to you by a physician?   Yes ___   No ___
If the answer is yes, furnish the details:

(Prior drug use will not disqualify you from consideration if you have been rehabilitated and are not currently using illegal drugs.)

GENERAL

Position(s) applied for	Date available for work

Nursing Applicants -- Please indicate clinical preferences:
1)   2)   3)

Applying for __ Full-time (80 hours per pay period or more) __ Part-time __ Temporary __ Casual	What shift(s) will you work? __ Days __ Nights __ Weekends __ PMs __ Holidays	Wage or salary requirements $

SKILLS

Clerical Applicants - Please complete this section

Typing: WPM _____   List any office machines/equipment you can operate:

Shorthand: WPM _____

All applicants -- Please list any additional experiences, skills and qualifications which relate to the job you are applying for:

Figure 4-1. Application for Employment, Page 1

Judie Knuth

Judie Knuth is employed as a Senior Staff Consultant for Firstaff, a St. Paul, Minnesota firm that provides professional office staff members to companies. In her position with Firstaff, Ms. Knuth is involved in the day-to-day operation of selecting and recommending high-quality employees. In this capacity, she agreed to give us some tips about filling out the job application form.

'The job application form is one tool that contributes to a hiring decision, represents you, and reinforces the adage, "What you see is what you get", ' Ms. Knuth explains. 'Employers expect the form to be legible, all the information to be accurate (with no misspellings), and all the blanks to be filled out completely. Always be thorough and give the information requested rather than stating "see resume". '

"Some tips to remember would be to review the form before you actually begin filling it out," Ms. Knuth goes on. 'This shows you can follow instructions. Keep a short "cheat sheet" in your billfold listing company names, dates, addresses, phone numbers, and reference sources. This sheet should always be updated as your career advances and will serve as a small portable resume.'

"Be aware that the length of time you take to complete the application is observed. Was it done quickly, but incompletely? Did it take so long you should not be considered for projects with short turn-arounds?"

"Anytime you are requested to list additional skills, take the initiative to sell yourself. When going to a company to fill out an application without a pre-arranged appointment, arrive before 10 a.m. This places you in the group of early birds who often get the worm ahead of their stay-in-bed competition."

"Remember," Judie Knuth concludes, "the job application form is only one step in your job search, but each step must be handled with top quality for the ultimate goal of employment."

- Education section

- Work history or employment record section

- Facts agreement section

- Reference section

THE PERSONAL DATA SECTION

The first section of most job application forms will ask for personal information about the applicant. This information should be filled in thoroughly and correctly. You should leave no line blank unless it does not apply to your situation. The following personal data is usually found on most forms:

- Full name

- Address, city, state, zip code

- Telephone (home and work)

- Social Security number

- Today's date

- Under the age of eighteen? (This is a legal question based upon insurance, bonding, and state and federal laws)

Information that cannot legally be asked of you on an application blank includes: age (other than the aforementioned), religion, weight, height, and national origin (optional information that can be asked on an Equal Opportunity Employment form, Figure 4.3, discussed later in the chapter).

Other information that may be asked in the personal information section of an application form includes the following:

- Have you worked for this firm or its affiliate before?

- Who referred you to this company?

- Do you have any close relatives working for this firm?

- How did you find out about this job opening?

- Are you currently employed?

- Are you currently laid off?

- Are you licensed to perform any professional service?

Questions concerning disability. Although employers are not allowed to discriminate against individuals with a disability, they may ask on the application form questions that pertain to your disability if these questions relate to their job description. In this situation, the employer may want to find out what arrangements should be made to accommodate your disability to the job description. The employer needs to know if there are any mechanical devices, furniture, climate conditions, or environments that meet your needs. Usually there is a short space on the application form for you to explain any special circumstances.

Questions concerning criminal records. Employers also cannot discriminate against applicants convicted of a serious crime (i.e., felony, homicide, etc.). However, they may ask on the application form if you were ever convicted of a crime and, if so, when. The reason this question is asked is based on the assumption that most employers have their employees *bonded* (the employer is insured against a financial loss or theft by the employee). If your past criminal offense is related in any way to the job description, such as theft, the company has the right to refuse to hire you. Some individuals fail to respond truthfully to this section and thus leave themselves open to facing automatic dismissal, should the employer ever learn about their criminal record.

Questions concerning drug and alcohol abuse. Finally, an employer may ask if an applicant has ever used narcotics or hard drugs not prescribed by a physician. If so, employers may not allow you in areas where you could be tempted, as in a hospital situation where drugs are stored. Many firms and companies have AODA (Alcoholic and Drug Abuse) programs that help their employees with these kind of problems. You may want to explain on your application form if you are being treated for any substance abuse.

THE GENERAL SECTION: JOB INQUIRY

The first question usually asked in the general section of an application form is "For which job or position are you applying?" Here you write or print the position that you found listed on the posting or want ad. For example: secretary, accounting assistant, salesperson, supervisor, etc.

Most application forms will ask you when you will be available to start work. If you are currently unemployed, you would obviously put down "immediately" or "when needed." If you are currently employed, you should check with your employer to determine what the proper notice should be. If you feel uncomfortable asking your current employer, a two-week notice is a good standard.

In the job inquiry section, you may also be asked for which of the following classifications you are applying:

- Full-time (40 hours or more a week)

- Part-time

- Temporary

- Casual (someone who would fill in on an as-needed basis, usually less than temporary)

Additionally, you might be asked what shifts you would be willing to work: days, nights, weekends, holidays. In some occupations, employees may work four ten-hour days and be given three-day weekends. In other jobs, employers will allow certain employees to "job share," an arrangement in which two or more employees share the forty-hour work week. Job share has become popular with working families because it allows a man or woman to spend more time at home.

What are your wage requirements? The wage requirement question can cause you distress. You do not want to price yourself out of consideration, nor do you want to ask for so little that the job would not be worth your time. A safe bet is to write or print "present rate." You can usually do some negotiating once you have been offered the job. However, if you must have a certain wage or salary, it may be to your benefit to let the employer know right away.

In the job inquiry section, the following hints may help you decide what information you want to give an employer:

1. Even though you want an employer to know that you can start work as soon as possible, do not let your previous employer down by not giving proper notice or time to hire someone else. KEEP PREVIOUS EMPLOYERS HAPPY. THEY ARE GOOD REFERENCES.

2. As mentioned in previous chapters, DO YOUR HOMEWORK and find out about salary requirements. If unsure, put down "present rate."

THE SKILLS AND ABILITIES SECTION

Employers want to know what skills and abilities an applicant possesses that relate to the job description, or which, in addition to the job description, would benefit the company. Examples of what employers are looking for include:

- Typing (speed and accuracy)

- Microcomputer hardware/software

- Shorthand/notehand

- Transcription

- Artistic abilities

- Foreign language

- Business machines/calculators

- Heavy equipment/machines

- Sign language

In the skills and abilities section of a job application form you may also be asked about your hobbies and interests. Some employers may find something you do that fits well into their corporate family. For example: A food industry sponsors a softball or basketball team. You may have a sport skill they need, even though it is external to the position for which you are applying.

As in the personal data section, the employer may also ask if you have any special licenses or certification. Usually this license or certification is granted by the state or federal government. Jobs that require a license or special certification include:

- Teachers

- Public accountants

- Plumbers

- Electricians

- Lawyers

- Doctors/dentists

- Nurses

- Cosmetologists/barbers

When it comes to special skills and abilities:

1. Do not sell yourself short. Remember such abilities as typing skills, computer skills, organization skills, mechanical skills, etc.

2. If you cannot think of any abilities and skills that are asked for, leave this section blank. It is better to be honest than embarrassed later when your employer discovers that you do not have the skill you listed on your job application form. Another alternative is to just list some domestic (home) skills or hobby skills.

THE EDUCATION SECTION

With the exception of your elementary school, you will need to know what schools you attended and when, to fill out the education section of your job application form (see Figure 4.2). If you attended more than one high school, list the last one you attended or the one from which you graduated. Look in your job application folder to recall what dates you attended or graduated. On the application form you will find the following columns:

- Name and address of school

- Years attended

- Last year completed

- Diploma or course of study

When the form asks for a course of study in the high school line, you may write: business, technical education, art, college preparatory, general education, etc.

In the education section of the job application, employers may also want to know if you received any special awards or academic recognition. You should list as many as you can remember, and include both high school and post-secondary awards. Again, refer to your application folder.

On some application forms, you may find under the school column a line that indicates "other." Here, list any seminars or workshops that you attended, especially as they relate to the job for which you are applying.

EDUCATION

NAME AND ADDRESS OF SCHOOL	YEARS ATTENDED	CIRCLE LAST YEAR COMPLETED	DID YOU GRADUATE?	LIST DIPLOMA DEGREE OR COURSE OF STUDY
High School	From To	1 2 3 4	___ Yes ___ No	
Business/Technical	From To	1 2 3 4	___ Yes ___ No	___ LPN ___ ADN
College	From To	1 2 3 4	___ Yes ___ No	___ BSN ___ MSN
Other (specify)	From To	1 2 3 4	___ Yes ___ No	___ RN DIPLOMA

Please list any academic or special awards you have received:

WORK HISTORY

PRESENT OR LAST EMPLOYER	Company Name		Employed From To	
	Street Address City State Zip		Telephone	
	Type of work	Last Salary ___ Full-Time	___ Part-Time	Name/Extension of supervisor
Reason for Leaving		May we contact for a reference?	Your name then (if different)	

NEXT PREVIOUS EMPLOYER	Company Name		Employed From To	
	Street Address City State Zip		Telephone	
	Type of work	Last Salary ___ Full-Time	___ Part-Time	Name/Extension of supervisor
Reason for Leaving		May we contact for a reference?	Your name then (if different)	

NEXT PREVIOUS EMPLOYER	Company Name		Employed From To	
	Street Address City State Zip		Telephone	
	Type of work	Last Salary ___ Full-Time	___ Part-Time	Name/Extension of supervisor
Reason for Leaving		May we contact for a reference?	Your name then (if different)	

NEXT PREVIOUS EMPLOYER	Company Name		Employed From To	
	Street Address City State Zip		Telephone	
	Type of work	Last Salary ___ Full-Time	___ Part-Time	Name/Extension of supervisor
Reason for Leaving		May we contact for a reference?	Your name then (if different)	

Figure 4-2. Application for Employment, Page 2

THE WORK HISTORY OR EMPLOYMENT RECORD SECTION

Usually, the work history or employment record section of an application form begins by asking for an applicant's most recent or present employment. The form will also ask for a history of work experience, in reverse chronological order. You should keep track of the following information regarding previous employers:

- Name, address, and telephone number
- Dates or hours you were employed
- Job description or type of work
- Previous salary
- Full or part time
- Name of supervisor
- Reference contact
- Reason for leaving

If you are just starting out in the work force, it is extremely important that you list all previous jobs regardless of whether you were paid or did volunteer work. Such activities as babysitting, lawn and garden work, snow shoveling, domestic engineering (raising a family), church volunteer, playground monitor, etc. may be just enough experience to get your foot in the door.

If you feel reluctant to list an employer or job with whom you had a bad experience, remember that you may be asked in an interview to explain any gaps in your employment history. It is probably better to explain to the interviewer your reasons for leaving a previous job than to omit the job from your work history altogether. If you had a bad experience with a previous employer, you may want to explain that your expectations were not being met by the reality of the job. This subject will be discussed in greater detail in Chapter 5.

What will be emphasized in other chapters of this text will be the importance of leaving previous employment with the best relationship possible. Prospective employers really like to check with the previous employers of serious applicants.

THE FACTS AGREEMENT SECTION

Most employers require an applicant to sign an agreement stating that the facts listed on the application form are true (see Figure 4.3). Some employers will also ask you to allow them to investigate credentials and qualifications. Any misrepresentation of these facts could lead to the cancellation of the application process, or, if already hired, dismissal.

THE REFERENCES SECTION

Employers will sometimes ask an applicant to identify on the application form people they might call to inquire about the job candidate's characteristics, work experiences, work ethic, personality, honesty, integrity, skills and abilities, etc. Your best references are former employers. However, if for some reason you cannot list former employers, you may want to list some of the following:

- Former teachers
- Coaches
- Personal friends
- Community leaders or business people who know you
- Clergy

AGREEMENT TO INVESTIGATION AND RELEASE

READ CAREFULLY AND ACKNOWLEDGE BY YOUR WRITTEN SIGNATURE AND TODAY'S DATE

I certify that the facts set forth in this application are true and complete, and I authorize investigation of the statements I have made.

I release from any and all liability all representatives of the Hospital for their acts performed in good faith and without malice in connection with evaluating my applications, credentials, and qualifications. I further authorize any party having information bearing upon my qualifications for employment to release such information to the Hospital (unless otherwise stated). I also release from any and all liability all individuals and organizations who provide information to the Hospital in good faith and without malice concerning my employment competence, ethics, character and other qualifications, including other privileged or confidential information.

I understand that any false statements or omissions concerning requested information on this application shall be sufficient cause for denial of employment or summary dismissal. I also understand that my employment at the hospital is contingent upon the satisfactory completion of a physical examination and investigation of my work record and references. I consent to a post-offer pre-employment physical examination and such future examinations as may be required by the Hospital. I further understand that, if employed, I will serve at least a 180-day probationary period from my date of employment.

I understand that if I am employed by the Hospital, my employment can be terminated by either the Hospital or me at will, with or without cause, and with or without notice, at any time. I understand that no one at the Hospital, other than the President, has the authority to alter, orally or in writing, this terminable-at-will status of employment.

_____   _____
Signature of Applicant   Date

NONDISCRIMINATION

It is the policy of the Hospital to consider all applicants for employment without regard to age, race, religion, creed, color, handicap (disability), marital status, sex, national origin, ancestry, sexual orientation, military reserve status or any other unlawful basis.

FOR PERSONNEL DEPARTMENT USE ONLY

REFERENCE CHECKS: SENT: RECEIVED   BY PHONE

                           1) _____   1) _____   1) _____

                           2) _____   2) _____   2) _____

                           3) _____   3) _____   3) _____

DATE APPLICATION RECEIVED:_____   DATE INTERVIEWED:_____

DATE JOB OFFERED:_____   DATE OFFER ACCEPTED/DECLINED: _____

JOB TITLE:_____   HOURS/PAY PERIOD: _____

STARTING DATE:_____   DEPARTMENT/UNIT: _____

WAGES/SALARY:_____   SHIFT: _____

COMMENTS·_____

ALL ENTRIES IN THIS SECTION MUST BE INITIALED AND DATED BY STAFF MAKING THE ENTRY.

Figure 4-3. Application for Employment, Page 3

Interests such as playing baseball in your free time can be a big plus to an employer whose company sponsors its own softball team. Be sure to list your hobbies and interests where requested on a job application form. (Photo by Mary Langenfeld.)

The number one rule regarding references is that you first ask permission from the people you want to use. In the reference section of your application form you will need to list three or four people. It is not appropriate to list fathers, mothers, or relatives. As shown in Chapter 2 of this text, you may want your references to write a letter of recommendation.

THE EQUAL EMPLOYMENT OPPORTUNITY SURVEY

The Applicant Equal Employment Opportunity survey shown in Figure 4.4 is included in this chapter so you are not surprised if an employer attaches it to your application form. The EEO survey is used by employers to help them consider minority or veteran candidates. As noted at the end of the survey, its completion is strictly voluntary.

SUMMARY

The application form is an important part of the job application process because, next to the resume, it is the employer's best opportunity to check your credentials to determine whether you are a potential candidate for employment. In addition, the job application form is also important because it is referred to by the employer during your interview, and is a means of learning about the accuracy of your information, your ability to spell and use grammar correctly, your military record, other data relative to the job, and your neatness.

There are seven basic sections of the job application form that is used by most employers. These sections are:

- **The Personal data section**—information includes your name, address, phone numbers (home and work), Social Security number, date, and whether your are under the age of eighteen.

```
┌─────────────────────────────────────────────────────────────┐
│                                                               │
│  APPLICANT EEO SURVEY          DATE _____          │
│                                                               │
│                                                               │
│  Position applied for: _____   │
│                                                               │
│                                                               │
│                                                               │
│  Sex:    [ ] Male                    [ ] Female               │
│                                                               │
│                                                               │
│                                                               │
│  Ethnic origin (check one):      [ ]    White (not of Hispanic origin)  │
│                                  [ ]    Black (not of Hispanic origin)  │
│                                  [ ]    Hispanic             │
│                                  [ ]    American Indian or Alaskan Native │
│                                  [ ]    Asian or Pacific Islander │
│                                                               │
│                                                               │
│                                                               │
│  Please check if you are:        [ ]    Vietnam Veteran      │
│                                  [ ]    Disabled Veteran     │
│                                                               │
│                                                               │
│                                                               │
│  Do you have a disability or handicap?    [ ]  YES    [ ]  NO │
│                                                               │
│                                                               │
│                                                               │
│  NOTE:  Completion of this survey is for statistical purposes only and is voluntary.  If │
│  completed, this information will be kept separate from your application and will not be │
│  used in any way to screen or select applicants.  Failure to complete the survey will not af- │
│  fect consideration of your application in any way.          │
│                                                               │
│                                                               │
│  Thank you for your cooperation.                              │
│                                                               │
└─────────────────────────────────────────────────────────────┘
```

Figure 4-4. The Applicant Equal Employee Opportunity Form Survey

- **The general section: job inquiry**—includes questions such as for which job you are applying, when you are available to start, what type of employment you are seeking (full-time, part-time, temporary, or casual), shift preference, and wage requirements.

- **The skills and abilities section**—asks what skills and abilities you possess that relate to the job description, or that in addition to the job description would benefit the company; it may also ask about your hobbies, sports, or interests.

- **The education section**—includes listing what schools you attended (except for elementary school) and when; it should be filled out with name and address of each school, years attended, last year completed, and diploma or course of study.

- **The work history or employment record section**—asks for a history of your work experience, in reverse chronological order, including name, address, and phone number of previous employers; dates or hours of employment; job description; previous salary; full or part time status; name of supervisor; reference contact; and reason for leaving.
- **The facts agreement section**—an agreement you must sign which states that the facts listed on you application form are true
- **The reference section**—the identification of people who might be called on by the employer to vouch for your job characteristics (work experiences, work ethic, personality, honesty, integrity, skills and abilities, etc.); the best references are former employers and the worst are family members.

QUESTIONS FOR REVIEW AND DISCUSSION

1. Employers feel the application form is as important as, if not more important than, a personal resume. Why?

   _____

   _____

   _____

2. What are the various sections of the application form? Why is it important to keep information in a job application folder?

   _____

   _____

   _____

3. What should you not do when filling out the application form?

   _____

   _____

   _____

4. Why do employers use application forms? What are they used for?

   _____

   _____

   _____

5. Employers cannot discriminate against you on an application form for a disability, a criminal record, or a drug or alcohol abuse problem. Explain.

   _____

   _____

   _____

6. If you were guilty of speeding, disorderly conduct, driving while intoxicated, etc. earlier in your life, should you list any of these offenses on your application form? Why or why not?

   _____

   _____

   _____

7. Why should you keep your current employer happy and give proper notice when you leave?

_____

_____

_____

8. What information do you need to document from former employers?

_____

_____

_____

9. Why is your father or mother not a good reference to list?

_____

_____

_____

10. What information should you keep in a job application folder:

_____

_____

_____

11. Some people seeking employment will walk into a firm, ask for an application form, fill it out, and leave. What is wrong with this scenario?

_____

_____

_____

CASE STUDY

Mike Doyle applies for the job of assistant manager of Burger's Department Store. He has just graduated from college with a two-year associate degree in marketing. Mike has applied for several jobs, but has not had an interview. He dresses appropriately for the job (white shirt, tie, dress pants, sport coat). His resume has been updated and looks very professional. Many people compliment him on his attitude and personality. Mike has admitted he made mistakes on the application form, but figures that his resume, which was done professionally, is excellent and should be considered over an application form. What would you suggest to Mike? Is the resume more important than the application form? Explain you answers.

PROJECT

Howard Johnson has filled out an application form for the job of Assistant Manager of Lake Dew Medical Center, as shown in Figure 4.5. Howard has made several omissions and errors. Take a red pen or pencil and circle all mistakes you think Howard Johnson has made on the application form. If you find eighteen or more mistakes, you are an excellent proofreader and you are very knowledgeable about the content of application forms. If you find less than eighteen mistakes, errors, or omissions, you should read the application form again and refer back to this chapter.

WORK APPLICATION

Company Name _Lake Dew Medical Center_

PLEASE PRINT OR TYPE ALL INFORMATION — USE ADDITIONAL PAGES IF NECESSARY

Last Name	First Name	Middle
Howard	Johnson	

Application for Position of:	Date Available
Ass. Mgr.	ASAP

Present Address - Number, Street, City, State, Zip Code	Home Phone (Include Area Code)
165 South Main, Minneapolis, Minnesota	234-6049

Mailing Address (if different from above) - Number, Street, City, State, Zip Code	Business Phone (Include Area Code)

What hours are you **NOT** available to work? (AM or PM)
Sometimes AM

What days are you **NOT** available to work?
☐ Monday ☒ Tuesday ☐ Wednesday ☒ Thursday ☐ Friday

Types of Employment Preferred (Check more than one box if desired)
☒ Permanent (Full Time)   ☒ Permanent (Part Time)   ☐ Temporary (Full Time) until _____   ☐ Temporary (Part Time) until _____

1. Do you have access to a car? (For some positions, a vehicle is required.)..................... ☒ Yes ☐ No
2. Do you have a valid driver's license?.. ☐ Yes ☐ No
3. Are you over age 18?... ☒ Yes ☐ No
4. Are you a U.S. citizen, or do you have an entry permit which allows you to work? .... ☒ Yes ☐ No

EDUCATION AND TRAINING

Circle the highest grade or year completed in school:
1 2 3 4 5 6 7 8 9 10 11 (12)+

Do you have a High School Diploma or a GED Equivalency?
☒ Yes ☐ No

Name and Location of High School
City High School
Minneapolis, MN

TRAINING BEYOND HIGH SCHOOL (College or University, Nursing, Business College, or other schools you have attended.) Under credits earned, indicate Q for Quarter Hours and S for Semester Hours.

Circle the number of years in College or University:
1 2 3 (4) 5 6 7 8

NAME AND LOCATION	Dates Attended From	To	Credits Earned	Major Field	GPA/Base	Degree (and Year) Conferred
City Business College	1990	1992	64	Marketing	2.5	Asso. Deg.
Minnesota Stat Un.	1992	1995	80	Bus. Adm	3.0	B.S.

Describe any education or training you have had which is not covered above, such as vocational school, correspondence courses, service schools, in-service training, or volunteer work which you feel is **relevant** to the job or jobs for which you are applying. Also include **relevant** licenses or certificates. **Be specific.**

Seminar - "Techniques For A Balance Diet"
Workshop - "Financial Planning For Retirement"
Workshop - Total Quality Management
Saminer - "Proofreading Techniques"

List any organizations you belong to (or have belonged to) and any job-related honors or awards you have received:
Rotary, Boy Scouts (Leader of the month - May)

ET-5011 (R. 07/92)

Figure 4-5. Work Application for Howard Johnson

WORK EXPERIENCE: Provide a complete description. This information will be used to determine if your application is accepted. *BE SPECIFIC.* Start with your most recent job. BE CERTAIN TO INCLUDE SERVICE IN THE ARMED FORCES. For part-time work, show the average number of hours per month. Indicate any changes in job title under same employer as a separate position. You may also attach Work Application Supplement (JET-5012) with additional information.

Employer Glen Lock Bar	Kind of Business Bar & Rest	Street Address 13 Brew Drive
Your Title Assistant Mgr & Bartender	Reason for Leaving Attend School	City, State, Zip Code Big Eppy, Wisconsin

Your Duties: Bartending

Total Time of Employed: 4 years — ☐ Full-time ☐ Part-time

From (Month & Year) Jan 1987 — To (Month & Year) Jan 1989

Check One: ☐ Monthly Salary Beginning: $ ☒ Hourly Salary Ending: $ 7.00

Employer Minnesota State U	Kind of Business	Street Address 1900 University Dr
Your Title Resident Hall Director	Reason for Leaving	City, State, Zip Code Rosedale MN

Your Duties: Direct Hall Activities

Total Time of Employed: 2 years — ☒ Full-time ☒ Part-time

From (Month & Year) Jan 1993 — To (Month & Year) Dec 1995

Check One: ☐ Monthly Salary Beginning: $ ☒ Hourly Salary Ending: $ 4.50

Employer	Kind of Business	Street Address
Your Title	Reason for Leaving	City, State, Zip Code

Your Duties:

Total Time of Employed: — ☐ Full-time ☐ Part-time

From (Month & Year) — To (Month & Year)

Check One: ☐ ☐

Employer	Kind of Business	Street Address
Your Title	Reason for Leaving	City, State, Zip Code

Total Time of Employed: — ☐ Full-time ☐ Part-time

From (Month & Year) — To (Month & Year)

Check One: ☐ Monthly Salary Beginning: $ ☐ Hourly Salary Ending: $

May we communicate with your present employer? ☐ Yes ☐ No

REFERENCES

Name Mike Smith	Address 80 Pokegama St., Big Eddy, WI	Telephone 726-4031
Name	Address	Telephone
Name	Address	Telephone

Figure 4-5. Work Application for Howard Johnson (con'd)

CHAPTER 5

The Job Interview

OBJECTIVES

After completing this chapter, you should be able to:

1. Explain how to adequately prepare for an interview.
2. State the interviewer's role in the job-seeking process.
3. Identify some important protocol for a job interview.
4. Develop good questioning techniques for an interview.
5. Discuss trends in pre-employment testing.
6. Explain important after-the-interview techniques.

THE IMPORTANCE OF THE JOB INTERVIEW

A **job interview** is the formal meeting between a job applicant and a representative of an organization. The formality of the interview often depends on the size of the company. In a small organization, you may be interviewed once by a manager or owner, and an immediate hiring decision will be made. Large organizations have human resource departments with personnel specialists. You may be interviewed by several people individually or by a group or committee collectively, and it may take two or three interviews and several days before a hiring decision is made. Regardless of the process, the importance of the interview cannot be underestimated.

The old saying, "Nothing happens until something is sold," is certainly true about a job interview. You are the product and the salesperson in an interview, and you must be prepared for this crucial part of the job search. Even though Fortune 500 companies have eliminated 4.3 million jobs since 1980, they, as well as smaller companies, are hiring every day. Jobs are available, but it is a buyer's market. You, as the salesperson, need to be over-prepared for this important job-seeking event. You must actively work to meet the major objective of a job interview—to get a job offer.

The job interview is your first opportunity to meet with an employer, or a representative of a company, fact-to-face. Come prepared and come with some enthusiasm if you want to make that all-important first impression. (Photo by Mary Langenfeld.)

PREPARING FOR YOUR INTERVIEW

Time and energy must be spent in preparing for your interview. Your self-presentation will usually determine whether you get a job offer. Preparation for the job interview is therefore necessary for people seeking an immediate vacancy, and it is also an investment that could lead to a successful career with a good organization. Good companies are made up of good people. Be prepared to communicate your values to the organization so you can provide a successful solution to the employer's needs. No matter how well qualified you are for any job, if you are not prepared specifically for the interview, you may lose your chance for a job offer.

REVIEWING YOUR RESUME

You have already developed your personal resume in Chapter 2. Now ask yourself these questions: Is this resume composed as well as it can be for this specific interview? If you were the employer, would you be impressed with the overall quality of the printing, paper, arrangement, etc.? If you have stated a career or job objective, is this position related to the objective on your resume? As part of your upcoming interview, make a final resume check to be sure it is as effective as you will need it to be to get a job offer.

Most employers concern themselves with the essential parts of a resume. They will use your resume as a reference to delve into your occupational and educational background, and your personal and professional activities. Be prepared to explain your involvement, or lack of involvement, in extra-curricular school activities. Employers like to see if you held leadership positions in any organizations. Be ready to emphasize past accomplishments, such as a safe driving award, or your strengths, like outstanding organization ability and excellent human relations skills. These characteristics are usually referred to as an applicant's "credentials."

Once you have checked your resume, find a conservative beige or gray folder or envelope for it. A manila folder with the company name printed on the flap is fine. Some prefer to call this folder a "job portfolio." This folder will keep your resume and other credential information neat, and create a good impression when you take it with you to the interview. Often, for one reason or another, the interviewer will not have a copy of your resume, especially when you are interviewed by more than one person. For this reason, bring at least three extra copies to your interview.

MATERIALS TO ACCOMPANY YOUR RESUME

In addition to your resume, you may want to include other credentials in your job portfolio. These might include:

- Certificate of recognition - 10 years of perfect attendance on the job
- Certificate of participation - Careers seminar
- Specialized certificate - Electronics technician
- Awards certificate - 2nd place—sales contest
- Employer evaluation - From previous employer
- Licenses - Real estate salesperson
- Letter of appreciation - Mayor's parking task force
- Work samples - Advertisements you created

Just one of these credentials, strategically presented, can set you apart from the competition and provide the edge needed to land the job.

RESEARCHING THE ORGANIZATION

It is always good interview preparation to learn as much as you can about the organization with which you will interview. You stand to make a much better impression if you can discuss intelligently some key characteristics of the company. This preparation immediately tells the interviewer that you have a keen interest in a successful job interview, and that you were motivated to seek out information about the company. All organizations are seeking highly motivated employees.

In doing your pre-interview research, focus on the following:

1. Know exactly where the organization is located and, if necessary, ask for directions on how to get there.

2. Find out what products or services dominate the company's business.

3. Learn what you can about the person(s) who will interview you. Be able to pronounce names correctly, and associate the persons with their job titles.

4. Know who manages the company, and, if appropriate, how the company's stock has traded over the past year.

5. Acquire whatever information you can about the organization's history and future prospects for growth.

6. Find out whether the company does business on a local, regional, state, national, or international basis.

7. From your research of the company, develop two or three questions you would like answered at your interview. Job applicants are almost always asked what questions they have for the interviewer toward the end of the interview.

If you are a student or a former student, your career services office may have information on several companies. You can learn a great deal from your career counselors about an organization's previous visits to your school. Many companies have brochures explaining their business, as well as annual reports. Most college and public libraries have a number of publications that provide important information about prospective employers.

Information about a company will give you a good foundation to work with during your interview. It will prepare you to make knowledgeable, intelligent comments and ask questions that demonstrate you are truly interested in the position. Your research on the company is your opportunity to put the final touches on preparation for a successful interview. Most of all, the knowledge you gain should help you to develop an attitude of self-confidence for the actual on-site interview. A positive attitude for you interview is a must.

EXPERT *Advice*

INTERVIEWING FROM AN EMPLOYER'S PERSPECTIVE

by Jeffrey Landsman

Many managers consider themselves great judges of character. Many fancy themselves experts in their fields. So why can't they hire good employees? Why do so many managers say "Good help is hard to find?"

The reality is that although many of us are fairly good judges of character and many are experts, among the best in their fields, we don't make good decisions when hiring our employees. Some of this is due to too much subjectivity; we tend to hire in our own image. Some is due to a poor or non-existent job description. But, I believe, most of the poor decisions in the hiring process are due to poor interviewing techniques. Too few companies train their management in the "art of the interview."

In this article, I would like to share some insight into the interviewing process, hopefully answering some questions and shedding new light on a somewhat nebulous skill.

Many people who conduct interviews for their companies think that the typical interview should consist of a series of boiler plate questions asked in a specific order with the same boiler plate answers being the only acceptable ones. The interview is considered to be a game of wits where the candidate is trying to sell his or her virtues and the interviewer is trying to find fault.

This is not a game though and, when prepared properly, can be used as one of the most valuable management tools for success.

Just as it is in the job description, the key phrase for a successful interview is preparation and planning. Like any business task, it takes time, trial and error and constant updating to construct a well prepared interview.

All interviews are not the same. Some interviews will be conducted over a period of time, and others will be finished after one session. The key to a good interview, though, is to be prepared.

Know what type of experience you are looking for. Be aware of the personality traits and image you want to have in your new associate. These are found in the job description you wrote. Have the questions ready that will elicit the answers that can qualify your candidate for the new position. Know the skills necessary and required for the job and find out if your interviewee has them.

Follow a specific plan and format for the interview. There is nothing worse for all concerned than a rambling lost interview that goes on and on without an end in sight.

Most interviews should contain the following.

1. An introduction which includes a brief period of small talk. Can the candidate make small talk? Is he or she the type of person you want? Will the candidate fit in?

2. A period for the candidate to tell you about themselves. This should not be a deliberate regurgitation of the resume, but rather an insight into the

person's background, what they want out of life and how they view themselves.

3. A question and answer period about your business and what exactly the candidate knows about it. Were they interested enough to formulate questions for you? Interested enough to do some research?

4. A review of the candidates resume or work experience. This along with #5 is the meat and potatoes of the interview. Has their past employment been a preparation for this job?

5. Some direct questions relating to the candidate's ability. Can they do this job?

6. A brief discussion of what your company does and what the candidate's job would be. Does this fit into their scheme of things? Do they want to do the job?

7. How the candidate can fit into the role and if they are interested. The final chapter. Will you offer them the opportunity, and will they accept based on the challenge at hand?

One of the things that we always ask ourselves as recruiters is can a candidate do the job, and does he or she want to do the job. There is no purpose of selling the candidate on the job or company (one of many first mistakes) if they have no interest. If a person has done their homework, they already have some interest in your firm. A matter of fact, if they are completely ignorant of your operation, do you really want them anyway?

I think that one of the most common reasons for high turnover is that the wrong people are hired in the first place. Often we become enamoured with a candidate because they are perceived to be the "right one" without benefit of an interview. Sometimes need is paramount to correct. Never make a rush, emergency hire under pressure or duress. Other than following a specific outline for an interview, the right questions also can be helpful. In order to make the right selection you should ask all candidates the same questions.

Questions can refer to the following: ability/suitability, time management, organizational skills, goal setting, self-image, communication and many other areas. Open-ended questions often uncover interesting responses. All avocations have their specific technical questions. The point is . . . ASK THEM!

Before closing, a few things should be noted. Not all questions are legal. Some basic no-nos are questions referring to age, religion, and race. It is best to read up on the EEOC before getting into trouble. An ounce of prevention . . . .

A good interview is the prologue to a good hire and an even better term of employment. Learning the art of the interview can be more important than almost any other function in your business, unless you work alone, of course.
Editor's note: Jeffrey Landsman is president of Roth Young Personnel Services of Washington D.C., an agency specializing in the hospitality and food service industry. He has more than 20 years of practical experience in the food industry, which he now puts to work in the personnel service business.

Source: *Food Service News, May 1993.* Reprinted with permission.

YOUR PERSONAL CHARACTERISTICS

In order to better prepare yourself for your interview, put yourself in the role of the interviewer. If you had to select one person from a group of four applicants, what would be important in making a fair selection? Some organizations make up a list of required and preferred characteristics and/or experiences for a specific position. Think of a way you could demonstrate each of the following characteristics during an interview. General personal characteristics may include:

- **Expressiveness**—Answer interviewer questions briefly and in a concise manner, including some questions that could be answered with a yes or no. Explain the yes or no if it will make your answer clearer to the interviewer.

- **Maturity**—Look the interviewer directly in the eye for most of your interview, but do not overdo it. Use eye contact naturally as you would when talking with a friend in a conversation. Applicants who lack maturity tend to lose eye contact.

- **Intelligence**—Listen for key points or questions the interviewer mentions, then summarize your answer by mentioning the point again.

- **Tactfulness**—Save note taking for after the interview, so you can give your full attention to the interviewer.

- **Courtesy and poise**—Be certain to thank the interviewers, for their time and consideration of you.

- **Confidence**—Conduct yourself as though you are determined to get the job you are discussing.

- **Dress**—Always dress in a conservative, no-frills manner.

- **Grooming**—Clean hair, hands, fingernails, and clothes are a must.

- **Sociability**—Shake hands with a firm grip, smile, and call the interviewer by name.

- **Decisiveness**—Be prepared to discuss how your well-thought-out career goals fit into the company's needs.

Evaluate yourself on these ten characteristics, and see if there are any improvements you might make before your interview. Study the list and add at least one additional point for each item. You cannot be over-prepared on these important personal characteristics.

YOUR PERSONAL APPEARANCE

Your first impression in a job interview is made when the interviewer sees you for the first time. The interviewer will immediately size you up and form a favorable or unfavorable opinion. Research has found personal appearance to be a number-one concern of interviewers. Appearance counts for 55 percent, voice 37 percent, and what you say 8 percent. You must consider the interviewer's concerns in preparation for your interview.

Different jobs dictate different styles of dress. If you are interviewing for a job as a waitron in a diner, casual dress is fine. Conversely, if the position is in sales for an up-scale retailer, conservative clothes are more appropriate.

It is best to play it safe when it comes to conservative dress for an interview. You cannot go wrong if you follow a few simple guidelines for women and men:

- **Women**—Wear a conservative blue, gray, or black business suit or dress. Your blouse should be white or a soft color like light blue. Nylons should be worn with a medium heel shoe.

- **Men**—Wear a conservative blue, gray, or black business suit. Say no to sport coats; they are too casual for a formal interview. Your shirt should be white or blue with a matching, conservative tie. Wear dark matching socks with black shoes.

A few additional guidelines should put the finishing touches on your preparation for a successful job interview:

- **Clean, pressed clothes**—Wear clothes that are fresh from the cleaners. It is a small price to pay for a successful first impression.

- **Clean, combed hair**—Wash and style your hair before an interview. Does it need a trim?

- **Beard, mustaches, and long shaggy hair**—Many conservative companies do not allow these. It is safest to cut off a beard or mustache, and trim your hair prior to an important interview.

- **Minimal makeup**—Conservative color and application protect your business image.

- **Trimmed fingernails**—Always a must, especially if you bite your nails.

- **Selective jewelry**—Bright and flashy jewelry distracts attention from your conversation and may project a slick or fake image.

- **Shined shoes**—Clean, shined shoes show attention to detail. They are an important part of personal appearance.

- **Clean glasses**—Clean glasses also show attention to detail. Glass smudges do not project personal cleanliness.

- **Perfume or cologne**—Use a soft-smell approach to perfume or cologne. A strong scent distracts from your interview.

- **Deodorant**—A job interview makes most applicants somewhat nervous. Pay close attention to personal hygiene.

It would be a rare case that someone who follows these points would not be well groomed to make a strong personal appearance for any job interview. You should make an excellent first and last impression by following these guidelines.

SOME ADDITIONAL INTERVIEW TIPS

After you have given close attention to your personal appearance, there are some additional factors that will enhance your prospects of receiving a job offer. Today's job market is extremely competitive because many people are out of work or seeking career changes. This buyer's market means employers can often be very selective and go beyond personal appearance and background when hiring new employees. To succeed in this environment, consider these additional tips to put you ahead of the competition:

1. **Go to your interview alone.** Bringing a friend projects a lack of self-confidence. If someone must accompany you, be sure he or she waits, out of the interviewer's sight. Also, bringing your children to an interview may be a major distraction for you and the interviewer.

2. **Be five or ten minutes early for your appointment with an interviewer.** If they want you to fill out an application blank, take a physical, etc., they will advise you of this procedure and include this time in your interviewing process, so there is no need to be too early. If you must be late, be sure and call with a good explanation.

3. **Do not talk in a derogatory way about former employers or teachers.** You will send a negative message to your interviewer.

4. **Do not wear lapel buttons.** Save your personal causes for another time and place.

5. **If you have to smoke before your interview, do it in an open area so your clothes don't smell.** Be sure to use a breath mint afterwards.

6. **Do not drink alcohol to settle your nerves.** Instead, take a high potency vitamin B capsule, drink some fruit juice, eat a high carbohydrate meal like

whole grain cereal with raisins, or have some pasta. Of course, caffeine colas, tea, or coffee will stimulate you for the interview.

7. **If your interviewer offers to shake hands, do so with a firm grip.** You may want to practice so you don't unknowingly use a limp-fish or bone-crusher handshake. Many people are unaware of the impression their handshake makes.

8. **Do not try to be funny and tell jokes.** Not knowing an interviewer's sense of humor can cause intended humor to backfire on you.

9. **Check your attitude.** Positive people are more convincing in an interview. Nobody wants to listen to excuses, complaints, or negative comments. Put on a happy face, regardless of how bad times may be for you, and be optimistic and cheerful for your interviewer. Everyone enjoys working with a positive co-worker, and you need to project this image.

10. **Fill out the application neatly and completely.** If you are asked to fill out an application blank before the interview, do so willingly and cheerfully. Some of the information on the application will be the same as what you have on your resume. Resist the temptation to write "See Resume" on the application blank. This shortcut might be interpreted as laziness or an unwillingness to follow simple procedure. (Refer to Chapter 4 "The Application Form."

In addition to these tips, consider the pointers in Figure 5.1.

Guaranteed Ways to Fail an Interview

- **Dress sloppy**—Wear a tee shirt that says "Working For A Living Stinks."

- **Undefined goals**—Tell the interviewer your major reason for working is to get insurance benefits and an early retirement package.

- **Talk too much about nothing**—Explain your training expertise by using your dog as an example.

- **Look around the room**—Comment on the poor choice of furniture in the interviewer's office.

- **Ask questions that are poorly thought out**—"When can I start dating other employees?"

- **Chew bubble gum**—Blow bubbles while the interviewer explains the company history to you.

- **Seem negative about everything**—Explain in detail why your last manager was a super bonehead.

- **Appear concerned only with salary**—Tell the interviewer money really, really motivates you.

- **Be unwilling to relocate**—Describe how your present relationship will prohibit you from moving, even for a promotion.

- **Seem to know little about the company**—Ask if the company is involved in any illegal activities.

- **Act dull and unenthusiastic**—Ask if you can catnap during any interview interruptions.

Question: Why are these points a guaranteed way to fail an interview?

Answer: They display poor attitude and preparation for the interview process.

Figure 5-1.

INTERVIEW QUESTIONS

When you really think about the job interview process, it consists mainly of a series of give-and-take questions. You need to be prepared in four areas of questioning: *interviewer, interviewee, illegal,* and *problem questions.*

INTERVIEWER'S QUESTIONS

"What will the interviewer ask me?" This question seems to bother applicants and it really shouldn't. With the right preparation you should be able to anticipate most of your interviewer's questions. Here is a list of questions that employers frequently ask during an interview:

1. How are you today?
2. Can you tell me a little bit about yourself?
3. Tell me, what is a [your name] really like? (Please explain yourself.)
4. What are your plans for the future?
5. What are your short and long term goals?
6. How long do you think you will be employed here?
7. Do you plan on being a manager someday?
8. Why are you applying for this position?
9. Why do you think I should hire you over someone else?
10. What makes you think you will be successful?
11. When are you available for work?
12. Why did you leave your last place of employment?
13. Why did you select our company?
14. Do you have any hobbies? What do you do in your spare time?
15. What do you know about this company?
16. Are you going on to school?
17. Have you had any experience in our type of organization?
18. What was the wage rate you received on other jobs?
19. What do you think of our company?
20. What were your favorite subjects in school?
21. What are your major strengths? Weaknesses?
22. Are you willing to put in overtime?
23. Do you get along with others—especially others who are quite a bit older or younger than you?
24. Do you have any pet peeves?

Although it is hard to guess what questions will be asked, you can prepare by developing answers to those on the above list. There are a few questions that especially seem to be favorites of interviewers. They are:

1. Why do you want to work for us?
2. What are your career goals?
3. What are your plans for the future?
4. Tell me about yourself.

Make sure you have good responses ready for all of these potential questions.

INTERVIEWEE QUESTIONS

Almost all job interviews end with the applicant having an opportunity to ask some questions. If you have none, the interviewer may think you are not interested in the company. You do not want to ask questions for the sake of asking, and you should not ask questions that may jeopardize your chances for employment. However, you do want to give yourself an edge over someone who is not prepared for this opportunity. Here are some good questions to ask:

1. Is it possible to advance to a higher position with your company?
2. Is there a chance to get into a training program?
3. What type of dress code do you have?
4. How do you evaluate employees?
5. What are your policies toward hair, beards, mustaches?
6. How has business been lately?
7. What is the company's transfer policy?
8. Are there any types of employee discounts?
9. When will I be starting, should you choose me?
10. Would furthering my education help me with your firm?
11. What is the starting wage? (Never ask at the beginning of an interview; some experts say it shouldn't be asked during the first interview.)

If your interviewer does not ask you for questions, wait until the end of the interview. Then tell him or her that you are very interested in the job and would like to ask a few important questions. Do not miss the opportunity to show your enthusiasm for the job and your excellent preparation for the interview.

There are also some questions that will jeopardize your opportunity to get the job. The following examples will cause an interviewer to question your intentions:

1. Do you really want me to start right away, or can I take some time off first?
2. When are your holidays and vacation days?
3. Do I have a start at a low level and work my way up to the top?
4. Who's the big chief around here?
5. I bet you make a lot of money, right?
6. Aren't most of your employees getting close to retirement?
7. Do I have to wear a suit and dress up all the time?
8. How many other people want this job?
9. Do I have to work overtime?
10. When can I join the union?
11. What do you think of me compared to the other applicants you have interviewed?
12. How much sick leave will I get, and how soon does it kick in?
13. Is it "OK" to date people who work here?

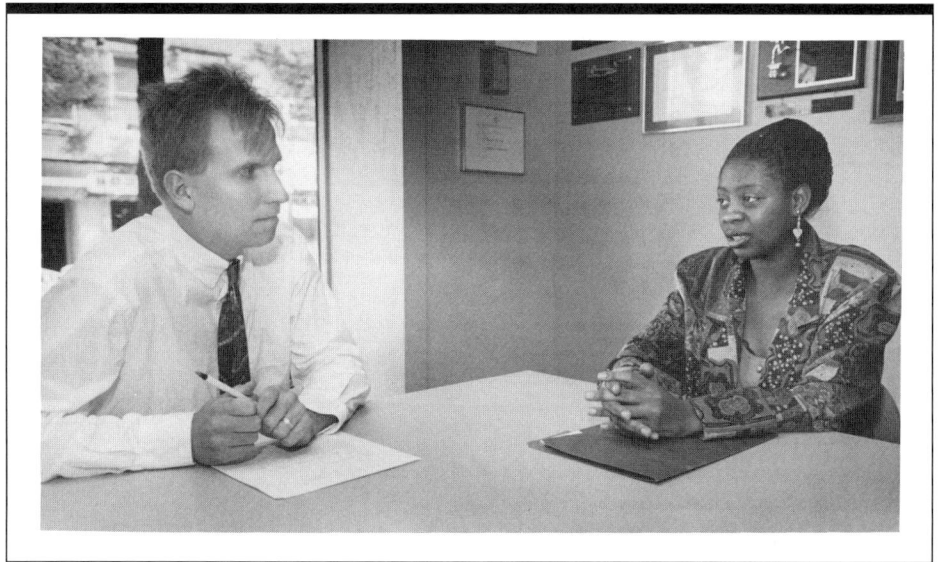

Be prepared to ask questions during your interview. If your interviewer does not ask if you have any questions, show your enthusiasm for the job by waiting until the end of your interview and then asking your questions. (Photo by Mary Langenfeld.)

14. When do we have company parties?

15. Who do I have to kiss up to for a pay raise?

16. Tell me about the retirement benefits.

17. When is the earliest date that I can retire?

18. Do you often fire capable people a couple of years before retirement?

ILLEGAL QUESTIONS

Equal employment laws protect job applicants from certain discriminatory questions. The protected areas all relate to an individual's personal life. Questions should not be asked concerning your birthplace, height, weight, marital status, number of children, dependents, pregnancy plans, sexual orientation, health condition, race, religion, housing situation, or age. It is also illegal to ask questions about someone's arrest record, but you can legally be asked about convictions. If a question is not directly related to the hiring decision, and not relevant to the job, it should not be asked of you. In the past, application forms had a place for a picture of you; it was not uncommon to attach a photo to your resume. The 1990s rule is no pictures anywhere.

If you are asked illegal questions, or asked for a photo, you will have to give considerable thought to an answer, and you may not have much time. Anticipate this situation and be prepared to politely ask, "Is this personal information important for you to make a decision about hiring me?" Most interviewers will get the message and drop the subject. Another school of thought says you should answer the question, keep the interview moving in a favorable way toward your employment, and try to correct the situation for future applicants after you get the job.

PROBLEM QUESTIONS

It is very likely you will not have the answers to all the questions in an interview. This is normal. Do not be afraid to admit the truth, or, in some cases, to simply tell the interviewer you can get the answer and telephone it back to the company.

         89

If you are asked a question like "How much money did your previous employer take in last year?" do not answer it. Simply say all financial information is confidential. The interviewer should appreciate trustworthiness and respect your confidentiality.

Most organizations like to pay you based on how much money you made at your last place of employment. If, during the interview or on an application form, you are asked how much you were previously paid, you need to answer honestly. If you are asked how much money you expect to make with a new employer, you may tactfully be able to avoid a specific answer. You can say you are open to the company's offer because you know they pay a fair wage, or that you are open for negotiations on salary. If you must state a figure, try to be a little higher than normal for the position. You can always come down to a lower figure, and you still might have a chance of getting the higher figure.

THE TELEPHONE INTERVIEW

The telephone interview has emerged as a major trend in the 90s. The use of this cost-saving approach is increasing daily. This interview technique saves employers the time and effort used in a face-to-face interview by screening the applicant pool down to a manageable number that they wish to actually bring in for an on-site interview. Using pre-arranged job requirements and desired personal characteristics, an applicant pool of sixty-five could be cut to eight for telephone interviews, and then to three for on-site interviews.

To earn an on-site interview, you need to be prepared to answer the kinds of questions asked in a phone screen. While previously mentioned questions are important, the following nine questions get right to the core of what employers want to know about you:

1. Why did you send us a resume?

2. Summarize your past work experience.

3. What do you feel most qualified to do with our company?

4. What would you prefer not to do with our company?

5. What are your work habits? Describe them.

6. Have you received any awards or other recognition for your past performance?

7. Can you highlight two or three of your professional accomplishments, and indicate how each would contribute to your performance as our employee?

8. In order for you to consider this position seriously, what salary would you expect?

9. Do you have any questions that you would like to ask us?

A conference call with three or four company representatives is often used to conduct the interview. One person will take the lead after introducing you to the other people on the phone, so your practice for this event need only be with one person, perhaps a good friend. Be sure to speak up and talk in a clear voice. Be friendly and let your positive personality show. Lastly, ask what the next step is for the company's hiring process.

PRE-EMPLOYMENT TESTING

Trends in the 90s make it safe to predict that many job applicants will undergo some type(s) of pre-employment testing. Organizations in business, education, and government often use tests before a job applicant is hired.

FITTING IN AT THE 3M COMPANY

Bob Walcott

Bob Walcott is the Division Controller for the Electronic Products Division of the 3M Company in Austin, Texas. In this capacity, he is involved in the hiring of new, entry-level accountants. In interviewing prospective employees, Walcott likes to determine how applicants would fit in and adapt to the 3M company. To do this, he pays particular attention to seven sought-after characteristics of new hires at 3M and to responses to ten questions concerning applicants' career goals.

Walcott says that the seven characteristics which 3M looks for in potential new hires are the following:

1. **Communication**—verbal and written; with individuals, to groups, with management

2. **Motivation**—incentive, drive, the need to succeed

3. **Assertiveness**—acting with confidence, a forceful or aggressive manner, leadership

4. **Poise**—tact, manners, positive interaction with people, the appearance of a professional, a good fit with the Controller's personnel

5. **Career Goals**—interest in the applicant's job potential at 3M rather than simply in the job itself

6. **Technical Expertise**—accounting ability, computer science aptitude and experience, work during school, campus activities, grade point average of 3.6.

7. **Business Sense**—entrepreneurial, innovative, creative.

To determine an applicant's career goals, Walcott says that he asks the following questions:

1. What are your long range and short range goals and objectives, when and why did you establish these goals, and how are you preparing yourself to achieve them?

2. What specific goals, other than those related to your occupation, have you established for yourself for the next ten years?

3. What do you see yourself doing five years from now?

4. What do you really want to do in life?

5. What are your long-range career objectives?

6. How do you plan to achieve your career goals?

7. What are the most important rewards you expect in your business career?

8. What do you expect to be earning in five years?

9. Why did you choose the career for which you are preparing?

10. Which is more important to you, the money or the type of job?

Walcott says that these questions are asked during the first thirty minutes of an interview session. At 3M, the company provides the following chart to interviewers so that a pattern of consistency is developed in interviewing all job applicants. While this division of interview time is applicable only to 3M, you should use this information as an example of what you might expect to encounter the next time you walk into an employer's office seeking work.

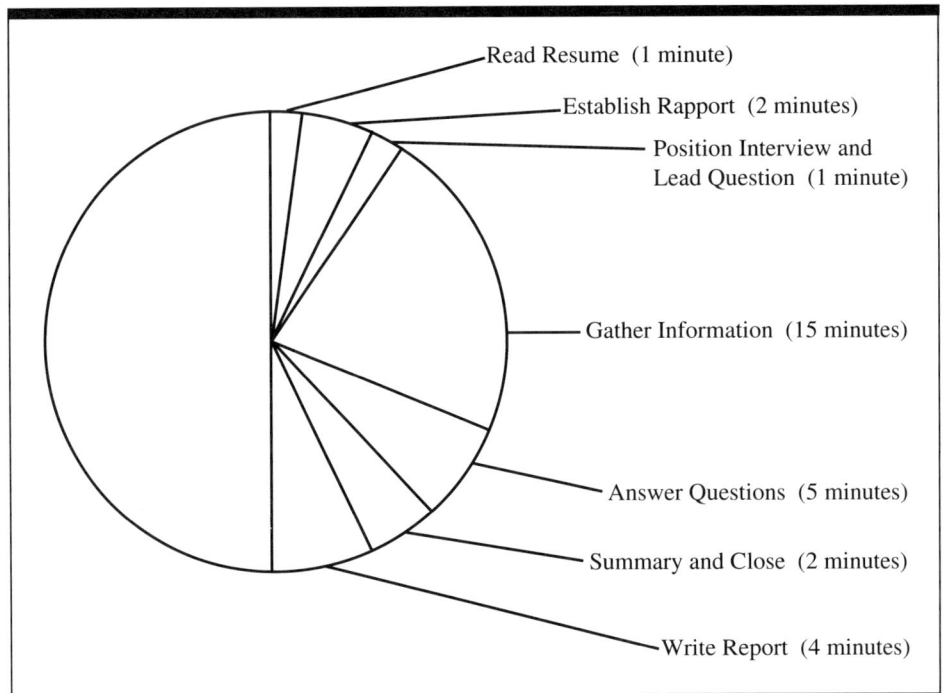

Read Resume (1 minute)
Establish Rapport (2 minutes)
Position Interview and Lead Question (1 minute)
Gather Information (15 minutes)
Answer Questions (5 minutes)
Summary and Close (2 minutes)
Write Report (4 minutes)

Components of the 30-Minute Interview

The purpose of pre-employment testing is to determine your strengths and weaknesses in areas of concern to the company; then employers will make a judgment on how well you will fit into their business plan. If you are weak in an area, it does not mean you will not get the job. No one is perfect. Employers know this and are often willing to train you or even send you back to school, or to a seminar, for a specific area of improvement, such as public speaking or report writing.

Before, during, or after the job interview you may be asked to take some tests. A wide variety of tests are available to employers from commercial testing companies. These tests can measure aptitude (driving a bus), intelligence (your IQ), skill (computer keyboarding), interest (child care), personality (outgoing) and even honesty and integrity if a polygraph test is given. In 1992, 40 percent of U.S. employers required substance abuse testing and 35 percent required some type of intelligence tests. These percents are increasing yearly at a rapid pace.

Some cutting-edge companies are using computers to prescreen potential employees. The applicant telephones an 800 number and the computer asks a series of pre-recorded questions. Answers are recorded by touching certain telephone keys for a yes or no answer. This self-administered test has proven more reliable than pencil-and-paper tests, or even polygraph tests, in research conducted at Mississippi State University. The computerized test treats all applicants the same and the results are not open to subjective opinions by the interviewer.

Passing scores are required before you receive an on-site interview with some organizations, and failing a pre-employment test can mean the end of your job search with that company. The pre-employment test importance can literally be anywhere from 0 to 100 percent, depending on the organization's viewpoint.

It will benefit you to try and find out what types of tests, if any, are given by an organization before you apply for a job. Be creative in seeking your answer, and do not be afraid to call ahead and ask someone in the human resource department. If you are nervous about what you learn, take additional steps to boost your confidence and increase your preparation. Visit your library for reading material on testing. You may also get some actual testing experience by taking a variety of tests at a local college, university, or state employment service. As a tax-payer, you may be surprised at the help available for the asking, or for a small fee, from these organizations.

A final point on pre-employment tests is the fact that scores can be used any way the employer so desires. This may sound discriminatory, but the fact is that tests are legal, including polygraph tests, which have been challenged all the way up to the U.S. Supreme Court. The lesson for the job applicant is to be as ready as possible for any type of pre-employment testing, because applicants who receive the highest scores on tests have the best opportunity to get a job.

COMPLETING YOUR JOB INTERVIEW

At the end of your job interview, several possibilities will exist. You may be offered the job and accept it. You may decline the offer. The interviewer may be frank and tell you that you will not be hired for one reason or another. In most cases, you will be told that a final decision will be made later.

Assuming a final decision later, you should know what the next step will be in the hiring process. Seek answers to the following questions:

1. Does the interviewer need any additional information about you?
2. Should you contact the company later? If so, when?
3. Will additional interviews be conducted?
4. When can a final decision be expected?
5. Who will make the final hiring decision?

End your interview by reaffirming your interest in the position. Do not be afraid to say something like "This has been an excellent job interview experience, and I would like to work for your organization." This ends the interview on a positive note for both the company and for you.

AFTER YOUR INTERVIEW

Every job interview is definitely a major learning experience for the applicant. It will help you gain confidence and prepare you for the next interview, should the need arise. You may want to take notes on how the interview was conducted. Just in case you are called for an additional interview, you may want to recall the questions, answers, and interesting facts of the first interview. Filling out the form in Figure 5.2 will help prepare you for your next interview.

Another important step after your interview is to send a follow-up thank-you letter. If any particular point or idea was not clear during the interview, include an explanation in your letter. The follow-up letter also gives you the chance to thank the interviewer for his or her time, reaffirm your qualifications for the job, and again express your interest in employment with the organization. Lastly, the follow-up letter is one more opportunity to keep your name firmly planted in the interviewer's mind. Your letter is a positive job-search technique. A sample thank-you letter may be found in Chapter 6.

 93

JOB INTERVIEW FOLLOW-UP AND NOTES

1. Explain how you found, and who referred you to, this job opening. How did you locate this opening?

2. How did you arrange for the interview?

3. Name of person(s) who interviewed you for your position(s).

   Name: _____   Position: _____

   Name: _____   Position: _____

   Name: _____   Position: _____

4. Review your entire job interview(s). Include how you got ready for the interview(s), what you said when you arrived at the business, what happened during the interview(s), the follow-up, etc.

5. List the important questions you were asked during the interview.

6. List the questions you asked during your interview.

7. List questions you forgot or would like to have asked.

8. List unusual or personal questions that took you by surprise or gave you difficulty in answering.

9. Was the interview as you expected? Comment briefly.

10. Describe the personal, technical, and skill qualifications the firm looks for in hiring for this position.

11. What qualifications did you possess that seemed to interest your interviewer the most?

Figure 5-2. Job Interview Follow-Up and Notes

A job interview is the formal meeting between a job applicant and a representative of an organization. You are the product and the salesperson in an interview, and you must be prepared for this crucial part of the job search. You must work hard to meet the major objective of a job interview—to get a job offer.

The job applicants of today must spend a great deal of time and energy in preparation for the job interview. Your preparation and self-presentation at the interview will usually determine whether you get the job offer.

Reviewing your resume is an important step in preparing for the job interview. It should be tailored to the specific position for which you are applying. Most employers will use your resume to delve into your occupational and educational background, and your personal and professional activities. In addition to your resume, you may wish to bring additional samples of past or current accomplishments to the interview.

It is always good interview preparation to learn as much as you can about the organization with which you will interview. You stand to make a much better impression if you can discuss intelligently some key characteristics about the company. Researching a company is an important job-search technique.

In order to better prepare yourself for a job interview, put yourself in the role of the interviewer. What personal characteristics and/or experiences would you seek in a new employee? Once you have determined these qualities, decide how you could demonstrate them during a job interview.

Your first impression in a job interview is made when the interviewer sees you for the first time. This is the moment that determines the interviewer's favorable or unfavorable opinion of you. Therefore, your personal appearance plays a key role in a job interview. Special attention must be given to the areas of dress and grooming.

When you really think about the job interview process, it consists mainly of a series of give-and-take questions. Many questions can be anticipated, and therefore prepared for before the interview. You need to be ready for questioning in four areas: interviewer, interviewee, illegal, and problem questions.

Pre-employment testing is a major trend in the 1990s. The job applicant needs to be prepared for a battery of potential tests. Special preparation must be done to assure successful completion of a variety of these tests.

Every job interview is a major learning experience for a job applicant. Certain questions should be asked by the applicant at the end of the interview. Another important consideration after the interview is to send a follow-up thank-you letter. You should also fill out a job interview follow-up form to be better prepared for your next interview.

QUESTIONS FOR REVIEW AND DISCUSSION

1. What is the significance of the fact that a job applicant is both product and salesperson during a job interview?

   _____

   _____

   _____

   _____

2. What is the major objective of the job interview?

_____

_____

_____

_____

3. Why must today's job applicant spend a great deal of time and energy preparing for a job interview?

_____

_____

_____

_____

4. Why should a job applicant review his or her resume before a job interview?

_____

_____

_____

_____

5. How will an interviewer most likely use your resume during the interview?

_____

_____

_____

_____

6. What are three examples of past or current accomplishments that you could bring to a job interview to promote yourself?

_____

_____

_____

_____

7. Why is it important to research a company before you interview with them?

_____

_____

_____

_____

8. What are three personal characteristics you feel would be most important for a job applicant to demonstrate during a job interview?

_____

_____

_____

_____

9. What determines an interviewer's first impression of you during a job interview?

_____

_____

_____

_____

10. What are three interview tips for a job applicant other than the areas of dress and grooming?

_____

_____

_____

_____

11. What are three examples of questions in each of these four areas: interviewer, interviewee, illegal, and problem questions?

_____

_____

_____

_____

12. What pre-employment tests can a job applicant anticipate from an aware 1990s company?

_____

_____

_____

_____

13. How can a job applicant prepare for pre-employment tests?

_____

_____

_____

_____

14. What questions should an applicant ask at the end of a job interview?

_____

_____

_____

_____

15. What should a job applicant do after the job interview is completed?

_____

_____

_____

_____

CASE STUDY

A local hardware store is looking for a new store manager. The store is affiliated with a large nationally known firm. This store has been family owned for thirty years, and now the corporation wants to take over the store. The family members want to get out of the business because they do not want to join the corporation. You are working for the corporation as a human resource manager and you are contracted to find a new manager for the store. Doug Blair is a 24 year-old college graduate whose major was marketing. His credentials are as follows:

- Graduated in 1994, B.S. Degree, B average.

- He worked in a hardware store for four years while going to high school and college.

- While in high school, he was convicted of possession of a controlled substance, which didn't affect his grades or his job in high school.

You had a one-and-a-half hour interview with Doug. He was friendly and understood the hardware business from a managerial perspective. You noticed when he first walked into the room that he had hair almost to his shoulders. He seemed to otherwise fit the qualifications for the job. As the human resources manager, will you hire him? Discuss your reasons for hiring or not hiring Doug with a partner. Be prepared to discuss your conclusions.

PROJECT

Look in your local newspaper and select a help-wanted ad that identifies a position of interest to you that is, one you feel prepared for in a practice interview situation. Pick a partner to act as an employer and interview for this job. Give yourself a few days to prepare for the interview. Ask your partner to pick some interviewer questions from the list in this chapter for your mock interview. Conduct the interview as if it were the real thing.

Your employer (partner) should use the rating sheet in the Figure 5.3 to check what you did right and also to note areas that need improvement. Save your discussion of this interview until you complete the second part of this project.

The second part of this project gives you the opportunity to complete a self-evaluation of your mock interview. After you complete it, sit down with your partner and really emphasize the points that will prepare you for a positive, successful job interview. Use Figures 5.3 and 5.4 as the basis of your discussion.

When seeking employment, "you will never get a second chance to make a good first impression." The employment interview will be the only chance you get. This interview should be a learning experience even though it is for practice. Strive to improve your interviewing skills and techniques by using the form in Figure 5.4 to complete a self-evaluation. Afterwards, discuss parts one and two of this project with your partner and look for similarities and differences on the two forms, with personal improvement as your major purpose.

INTERVIEWER RATING FORM

Name:

Position applied for:

	Excellent	Very Good	Good	Fair	Total
1. Expressiveness	10 9	8 7 6	5 4 3	2 1	_____
2. Maturity	10 9	8 7 6	5 4 3	2 1	_____
3. Intelligence	10 9	8 7 6	5 4 3	2 1	_____
4. Tactfulness	10 9	8 7 6	5 4 3	2 1	_____
5. Goal Oriented	10 9	8 7 6	5 4 3	2 1	_____
6. Confidence and Poise	10 9	8 7 6	5 4 3	2 1	_____
7. Appearance	10 9	8 7 6	5 4 3	2 1	_____
8. Sociability	10 9	8 7 6	5 4 3	2 1	_____
9. Positive Attitude	10 9	8 7 6	5 4 3	2 1	_____
10. Desire for Job	10 9	8 7 6	5 4 3	2 1	_____

TOTAL — 100 POSSIBLE   _____

Comments:

Figure 5-3. Interviewer Rating Form

INTERVIEW SELF-EVALUATION FORM

	Very Good	Good	Needs Improvement
a. On time for the interview			
b. Appropriately groomed			
c. Prepared mentally and physically for the interview			
d. Introduced yourself properly and politely			
e. Completed application form neatly and accurately			
f. Attentive during interview — good eye contact			
g. Displayed interest and enthusiasm during the interview			
h. Possessed confidence and poise			
i. Gave definite responses to questions			
j. Asked pertinent questions about the job and the company			
k. Handled unusual questions with ease			
l. Demonstrated the ability to express yourself clearly			
m. Exhibited knowledge regarding products, services, company or industry			
n. Courteous and well mannered at all times			
o. Presented qualifications for the job			
p. Prepared to answer personal questions			
q. Refrained from displaying annoying mannerisms			
r. Prepared to give good account of leisure activities			
s. Gave frank answers concerning school achievement			
t. Used previous work experience to advantage			
u. Expressed appreciation for interviewer's time			
v. Terminated interview with ease and confidence			

Other comments:

Figure 5-4. Interview Self-Evaluation Form

After the Interview

OBJECTIVES

After completing this chapter, you should be able to:

1. Explain the importance of continuing the job-seeking process.

2. Determine how well you performed in the job interview.

3. Develop an interview thank-you letter.

4. Write a not-interested thank-you letter.

5. Compose a letter acknowledging a job offer.

6. Send a letter accepting a job offer.

7. Send a letter declining a job offer.

8. Conduct a proper follow-up to the job interview.

WHERE DO YOU STAND?

The job interview gave you an excellent opportunity to display your positive attitude and discuss your past educational/occupational experiences. The employer was interested enough in you that time, effort, and expense money for the interview were spent on your behalf. Both parties have a mutual interest, and the question now is, "Where do you stand?" Several possibilities requiring some type of follow-up are normal at this point in the employment process; however, your first concern should be an in-depth self-evaluation.

SELF-EVALUATION

After your interview, do a conscientious same-day self-evaluation of your performance. In writing, list your strengths and weaknesses by filling out the self-evaluation chart shown in Figure 6.1, and start preparing for an even better interview next time. Think about improvements in any areas your interviewer may have questioned, verbally or through body language. Be creative, and search for possible improvements in the important areas of confidence, enthusiasm, poise, dress, language skills, positive attitude, and career goals. Lastly, was there anything good about yourself that you forgot to tell the interviewer?

Completing a job interview is not your final step in the job search process. Once you have said goodbye to your interviewer, it is important that you go home and evaluate your performance and write a follow-up thank-you letter. (Photo by Mary Langfeld.)

THE THANK-YOU LETTER

The possibility always exists that you will receive a job offer on the first interview, accept the offer, and have no further need for follow-up activities. In most instances, however, the employer is considering several applicants, and you will have a period of time to wait for an answer.

There are several excellent reasons to send a thank-you letter within two or three days after your interview. The **thank-you letter** is a kind and conscientious effort on your part to express your gratitude to an employer for granting you an interview. It also:

- Sets you apart from other applicants who may fail to send a letter.

- Demonstrates your understanding of good business and personal etiquette.

- Tells the interviewer that you are still interested, or possibly are no longer interested, in the job. If you are not interested, your letter clearly shows that you understand business ethics. Who knows—in the future you may want to reapply for a job with the same company. Do not "burn any bridges" between yourself and a potential employer.

- Gives you another chance to highlight one or two reasons why you want to work for the organization.

Your interview should be a learning experience whether you get the job or not. Strive to improve your interviewing skills and techniques because your future may depend on them. Using the following chart, evaluate yourself on the various aspects of your interview. Be objective and use the evaluation in preparing for future interviews. You may use this questionnaire more than once by making check marks with different colored pens.

	Excellent	Good	Needs Work
1. On time for the interview			
2. Appropriately groomed for the interview			
3. Prepared mentally and physically for the interview			
4. Introduced yourself properly and politely			
5. Completed application form neatly and accurately			
6. Attentive during interview - good eye contact			
7. Displayed interest and enthusiasm during the interview			
8. Possessed confidence and poise			
9. Gave definite responses to questions			
10. Asked pertinent questions about the job and the company			
11. Handled unusual questions with ease			
12. Demonstrated the ability to express self clearly			
13. Exhibited knowledge regarding products, services, company or industry			
14. Courteous and well mannered at all times			
15. Presented qualifications for the job			
16. Prepared to answer personal questions			
17. Refrained from displaying annoying mannerisms			
18. Prepared to give a good account of leisure activities			
19. Gave frank answers concerning school achievement			
20. Used previous work experience to advantage			
21. Expressed appreciation for interviewer's time			
22. Terminated interview with ease and confidence			
23. Determined what happens next			

Figure 6-1. Post-Interview Self-Evaluation Form

- Offers you the opportunity to mention anything important that you forgot to mention during the interview.
- Keeps your name actively in front of the interviewer.

THE PREPARATION OF YOUR THANK-YOU LETTER

The thank-you letter should be brief and to the point. Depending on whether you want a formal or informal presentation, you need to decide on a one-, two-, or three-paragraph letter. Following are descriptions and examples of each paragraph in a formal three-paragraph thank-you letter. You may wish to select parts of these three paragraphs for use in developing a shorter, more informal, thank-you letter.

PARAGRAPH ONE

Your opening sentence, as shown in Figure 6.2, should explain your reason for writing, which is to express thanks for the interview. The second sentence should mention something complimentary about the interview. This should be a sincere statement concerning something positive you saw or did. Examples could be a tour you took, high technology equipment in use, or people you met.

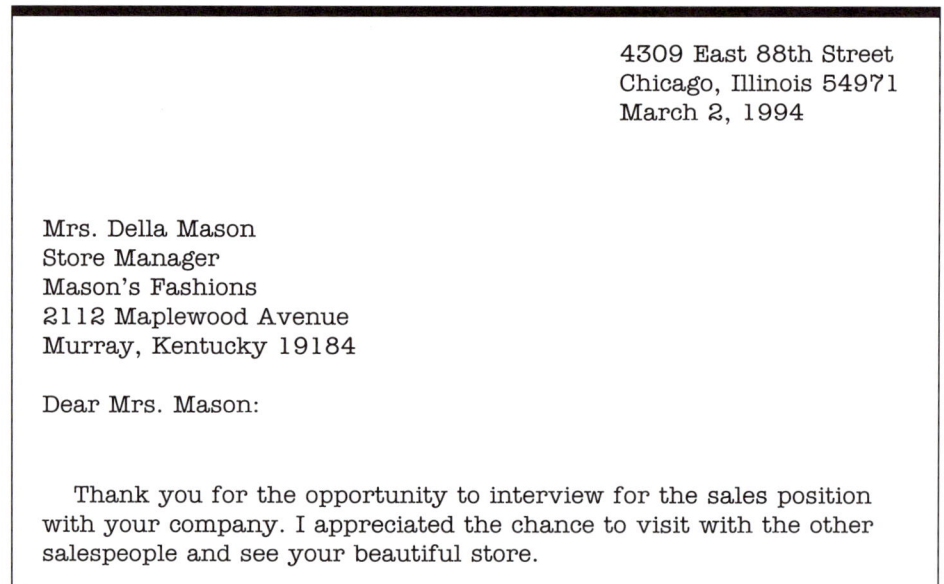

```
                                      4309 East 88th Street
                                      Chicago, Illinois 54971
                                      March 2, 1994




Mrs. Della Mason
Store Manager
Mason's Fashions
2112 Maplewood Avenue
Murray, Kentucky 19184


Dear Mrs. Mason:


    Thank you for the opportunity to interview for the sales position
with your company. I appreciated the chance to visit with the other
salespeople and see your beautiful store.
```

Figure 6-2. Paragraph One of a Thank-You Letter

PARAGRAPH TWO

The second paragraph of your thank-you letter, as illustrated in Figure 6.3, should reaffirm your interest in the position available and briefly explain your reasons. If you did not mention something important in the interview, include it here. Try to use an example that shows how something in your background relates to the employer's position. Build a bridge between you and the job.

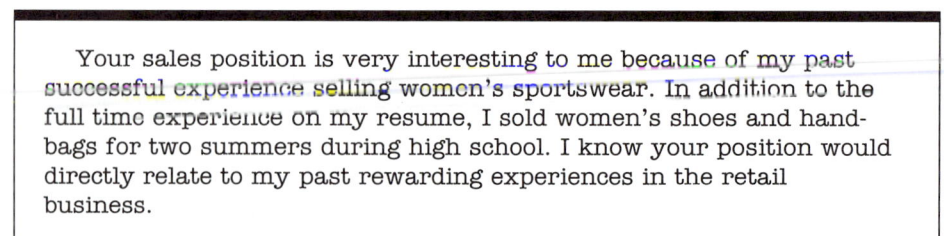

```
    Your sales position is very interesting to me because of my past
successful experience selling women's sportswear. In addition to the
full time experience on my resume, I sold women's shoes and hand-
bags for two summers during high school. I know your position would
directly relate to my past rewarding experiences in the retail
business.
```

Figure 6-3. Paragraph Two of a Thank-You Letter

PARAGRAPH THREE

In the third paragraph of your letter, as shown in Figure 6.4, you may add a sentence expressing your desire to send any additionally needed information. Be sure to include a final expression of thanks for your interview. Since you are still interested in the job, include an action statement that strongly conveys this feeling to the employer.

> Please contact me if you need any additional information about my background or references. Again, thank you for the interview. I will anxiously await your reply.

Figure 6-4. Paragraph Three of a Thank-You Letter

The three paragraphs of your letter should flow into a smooth, sincere expression of your feelings about the job interview and about your intentions to continue seeking employment with the company. The completed letter, as shown in Figure 6.5, meets the objectives of being brief and concise, as well as using a format that has eye appeal.

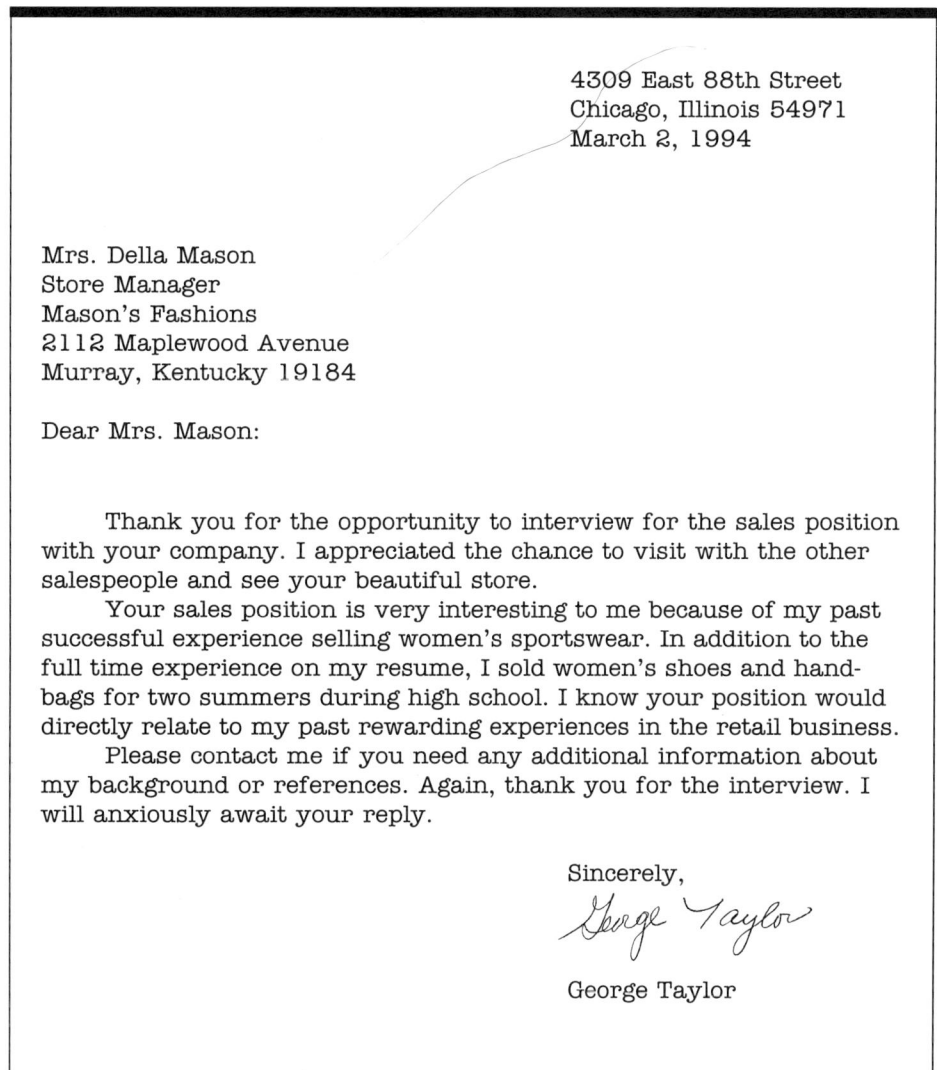

4309 East 88th Street
Chicago, Illinois 54971
March 2, 1994

Mrs. Della Mason
Store Manager
Mason's Fashions
2112 Maplewood Avenue
Murray, Kentucky 19184

Dear Mrs. Mason:

Thank you for the opportunity to interview for the sales position with your company. I appreciated the chance to visit with the other salespeople and see your beautiful store.

Your sales position is very interesting to me because of my past successful experience selling women's sportswear. In addition to the full time experience on my resume, I sold women's shoes and handbags for two summers during high school. I know your position would directly relate to my past rewarding experiences in the retail business.

Please contact me if you need any additional information about my background or references. Again, thank you for the interview. I will anxiously await your reply.

Sincerely,

George Taylor

George Taylor

Figure 6-5. The Complete Interview Thank-You Letter

THE NOT-INTERESTED THANK-YOU LETTER

Suppose you think about your recent job interview for a couple of days and decide the job is not for you. It is a good, courteous idea to send a not-interested thank-you letter to the employer. The major reason for this action is to preserve your reputation with this employer in case you want to apply for another job with the company in the future. In today's job market you never know what your needs will be in years to come. If you leave a bad impression with an interviewer, it could come back to haunt you. Some business fields are relatively small, and many employers, even on a national basis, know each other through professional associations. If your name is mentioned, you certainly want it to be in a positive way.

Figure 6.6 illustrates an example of a not-interested thank-you letter. Note the different second paragraph from Figure 6.3. Note also that there is no need for a third paragraph. Again, this letter is brief and sincere.

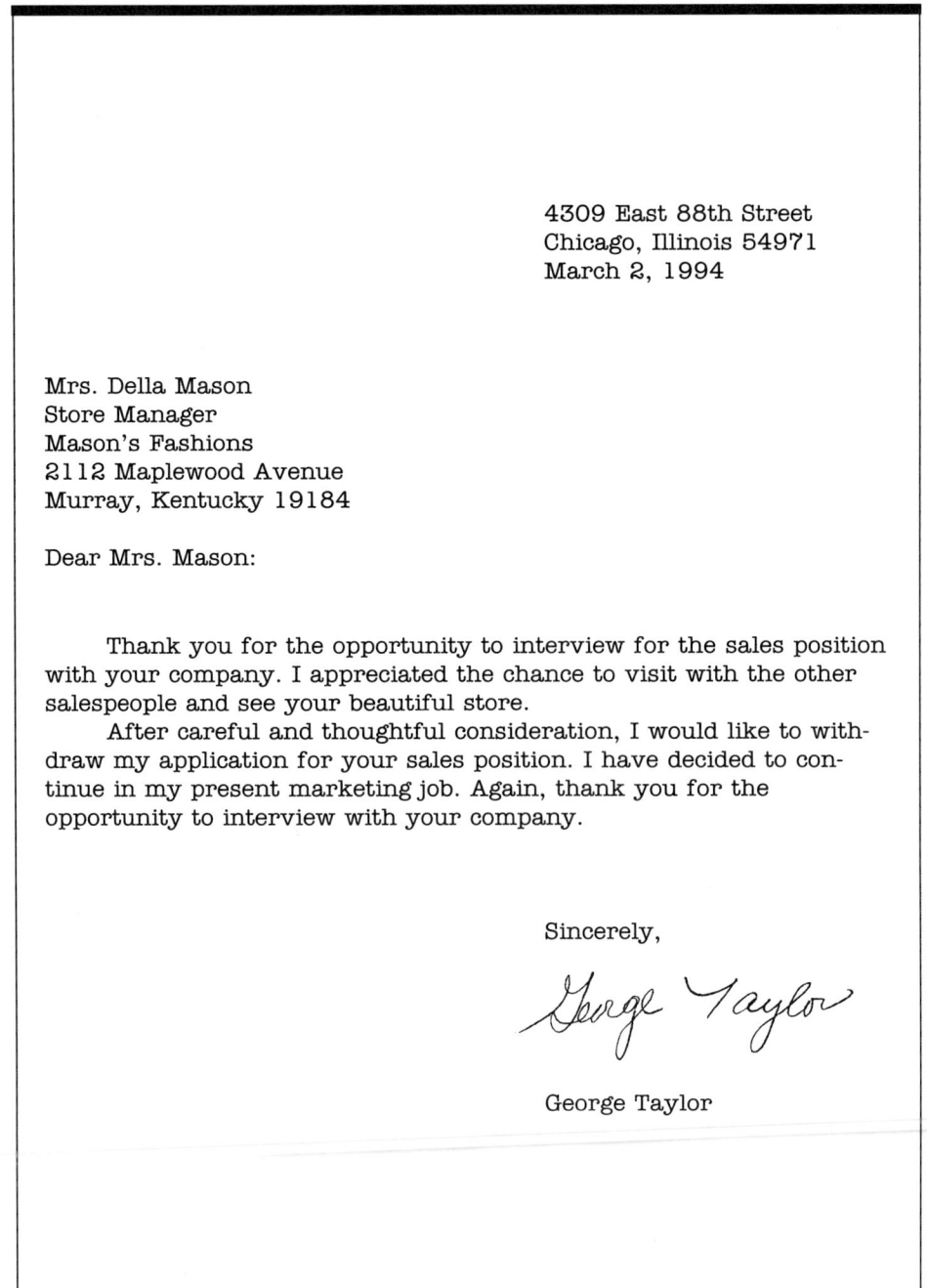

4309 East 88th Street
Chicago, Illinois 54971
March 2, 1994

Mrs. Della Mason
Store Manager
Mason's Fashions
2112 Maplewood Avenue
Murray, Kentucky 19184

Dear Mrs. Mason:

Thank you for the opportunity to interview for the sales position with your company. I appreciated the chance to visit with the other salespeople and see your beautiful store.

After careful and thoughtful consideration, I would like to withdraw my application for your sales position. I have decided to continue in my present marketing job. Again, thank you for the opportunity to interview with your company.

Sincerely,

George Taylor

George Taylor

Figure 6-6. The Not-Interested Thank-You Letter

THE LETTER ACKNOWLEDGING A JOB OFFER

Once a company has made an official job offer, usually by telephone or mail, you will want to respond immediately, even when the company gives you a few days or weeks to consider the offer by letter. Your objective is a return letter to thank the company for the offer and let them know when you plan to give an answer. Most companies will give you some time to think about a new position before you have to say yes or no. Figure 6.7 provides a brief and concise example of an acknowledgment letter.

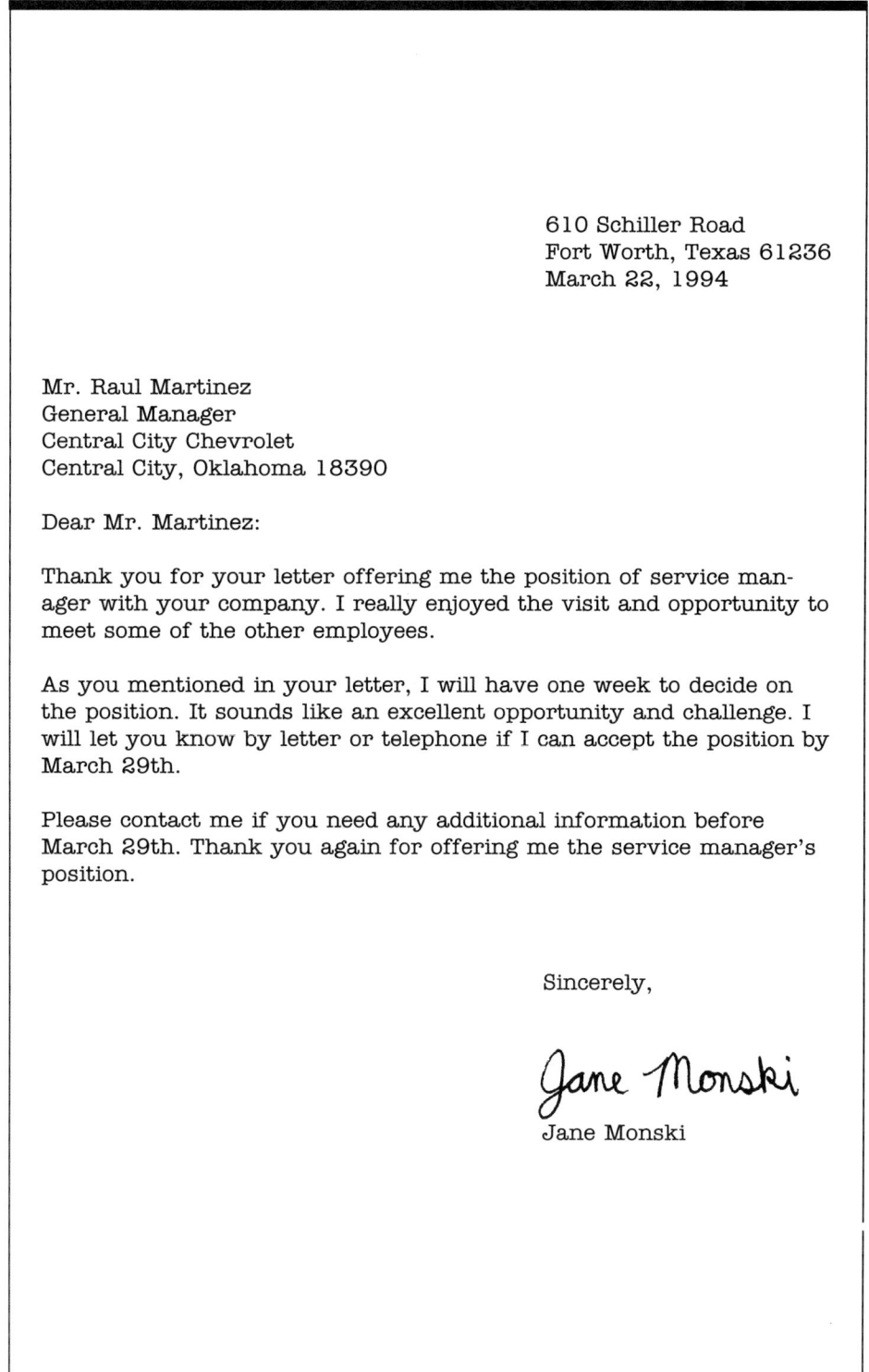

610 Schiller Road
Fort Worth, Texas 61236
March 22, 1994

Mr. Raul Martinez
General Manager
Central City Chevrolet
Central City, Oklahoma 18390

Dear Mr. Martinez:

Thank you for your letter offering me the position of service manager with your company. I really enjoyed the visit and opportunity to meet some of the other employees.

As you mentioned in your letter, I will have one week to decide on the position. It sounds like an excellent opportunity and challenge. I will let you know by letter or telephone if I can accept the position by March 29th.

Please contact me if you need any additional information before March 29th. Thank you again for offering me the service manager's position.

Sincerely,

Jane Monski

Jane Monski

Figure 6-7. The Letter Acknowledging a Job Offer

THE LETTER ACCEPTING A JOB OFFER

Many employers will make a job offer by telephone; when you accept over the phone, they will ask you to send them a letter formally accepting the offer. It is also very common to receive the initial offer by mail. In either case, you should be excited about writing a letter to accept a company's offer. Make sure you let it be known that you are happy to accept the new position and enthusiastic about starting to work. An example of an acceptance letter is shown in Figure 6.8.

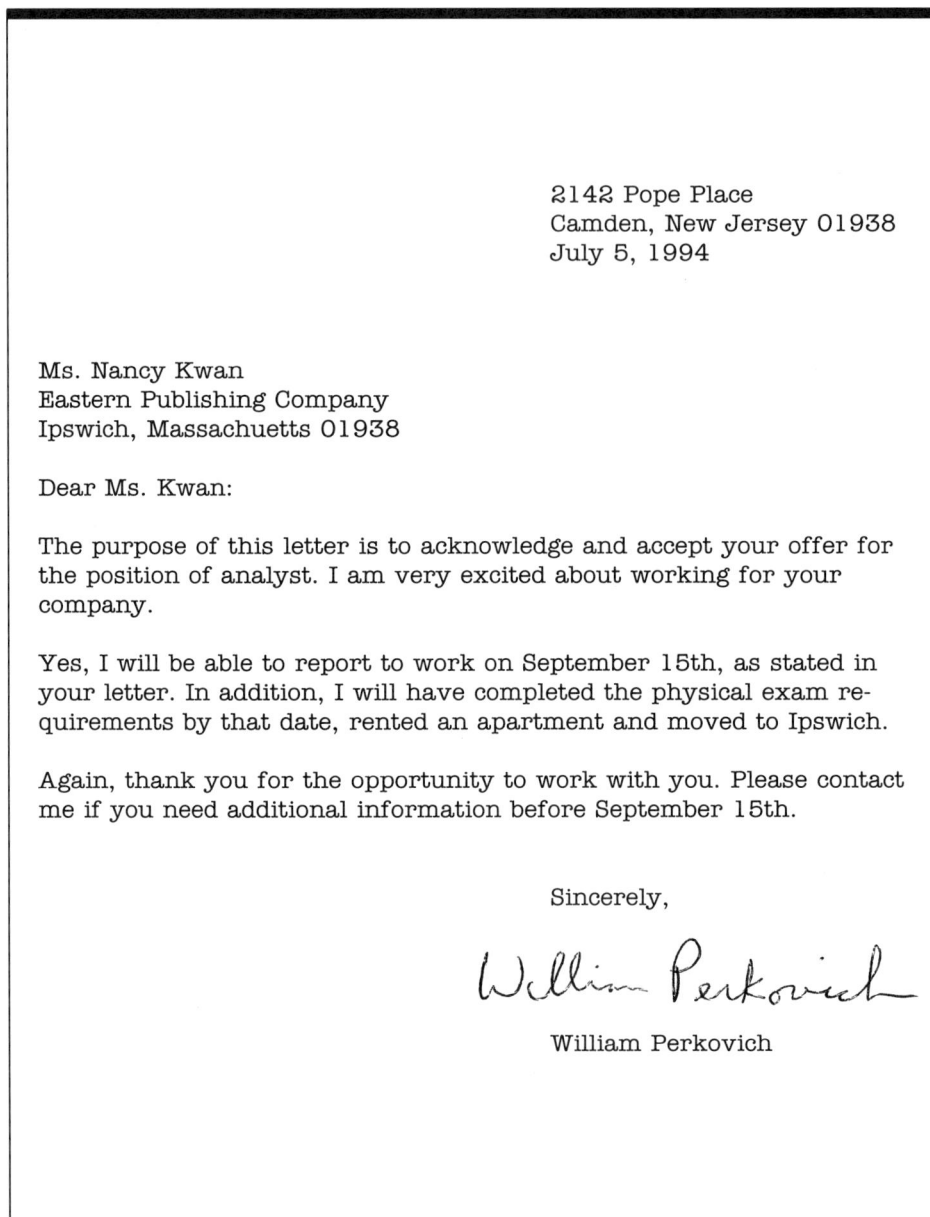

2142 Pope Place
Camden, New Jersey 01938
July 5, 1994

Ms. Nancy Kwan
Eastern Publishing Company
Ipswich, Massachuetts 01938

Dear Ms. Kwan:

The purpose of this letter is to acknowledge and accept your offer for the position of analyst. I am very excited about working for your company.

Yes, I will be able to report to work on September 15th, as stated in your letter. In addition, I will have completed the physical exam requirements by that date, rented an apartment and moved to Ipswich.

Again, thank you for the opportunity to work with you. Please contact me if you need additional information before September 15th.

Sincerely,

William Perkovich

William Perkovich

Figure 6-8. The Letter Accepting a Job Offer

THE LETTER DECLINING A JOB

It is a great compliment to receive a job offer, but sometimes you know the job just is not right for you and you must decline. Here again, you want to take proper action and tactfully keep future options open. It is always a good idea to compliment the employer, thank the interviewers, and give a reason why you declined the position. Figure 6.9 provides an example of a proper way to decline a job offer.

828 Bouchette Drive
Riviere Du Loup, Quebec
June 15, 1994

Ms. Sandee Stenwall
Human Resources Manager
The Kyle Kompany
315 Woodside
Advocate Harbour, Nova Scotia

Dear Ms. Stenwall:

After considerable thought and discussion with family and business associates, I have decided not to accept your offer of employment. This was not an easy decision for me, but I feel another opportunity matches my interests and qualifications better at this stage of my career.

I was very impressed with your company operation and professional way of doing things. The employees that I met were very friendly and extended a warm welcome to me. Thank you for the time and effort you spent considering me.

Sincerely,

Monique Neuville

Monique Neuville

Figure 6-9. The Letter Declining a Job Offer

THE TELEPHONE FOLLOW-UP

It is a good idea to follow up your interview with a telephone call. Organizations that check your references will need some time after the interview to complete the process. A good rule of thumb is to allow approximately six business days before you follow up by telephone. Then, speak to one of the persons who interviewed you. Let them know you are still interested in the position and ask if any additional information is needed. Ask when you can expect to hear from them, and thank them for their time and consideration. These procedures demonstrate your continued enthusiasm for the job.

REVISITING THE EMPLOYER

Circumstances may deem it appropriate for you to revisit an employer after the interview. For example, you may personally know the employer from a civic or professional organization. Or the interviewer or company may be located close to where you live. These conditions make it perfectly legitimate for you to stop in and check on the hiring process. Your visit demonstrates your continued interest in the position by keeping your image firmly implanted in the employer's mind. This type of determination has often proven successful. Use the same guidelines for the visit as you would in the telephone follow-up.

Revisiting a prospective employer after your interview is a good way to keep yourself in the employer's mind. (Photo by Mary Langenfeld.)

EXPERT *Advice*

INCREASE YOUR EMPLOYABILITY

Long story short. You need a job. Whether it's a proud new sheepskin or a dreaded pink slip that has plunged you into the chilly waters of today's job market, you can put yourself ahead of the pack by taking some advice from Harvey B. Mackay, an entrepreneur whose company in Minneapolis manufactures 10 million envelopes a day. ("I love the industry," he says. "People can only use an envelope once.")

Even successful, well-connected business owners can get "fired," as he found out when his bankers of 20 years kicked him out, without notice.

"A corporation is a lousy thing to fall in love with, because it won't love you back," he writes in the first chapter of his book, *Sharkproof: Get the Job You Want, Keep the Job You Love . . . In Today's Frenzied Job Market.* "You're never in the comfort zone, no matter what you think your position is . . . . Firings used to be done with surgical cleanliness. Now they're called restructurings, and they're done with a meat cleaver . . . . Serial killers are on the loose, hacking away at every corporate personnel roster in the land."

The new college graduate and the newly fired middle manager are both facing a whole new ball game, Mackay says.

"It's just unbelievable. In every industry, there have been more changes in the past four or five years than in the previous 20 years," Mackay says. "In 1988 alone, there were 3,500 mergers and acquisitions. Since 1980, 35 percent to 40 percent of *Fortune* 500 companies have disappeared. In 1991, 187 banks went belly up. One out of five Americans had their banks acquired in the past 12 months."

A high class ranking from a top-notch college or professional school is no longer an automatic passport to a great job, or any job. Impeccable credentials and an impressive résumé are no longer enough. Today's job hunter has to be a "hungry fighter," Mackay says, and looking for a job must be a full-time job that engages all the creativity and resourcefulness you can muster.

It gets worse.

Once you've landed the job you want, you really can't expect to keep it.

"You won't be sticking around to get the gold watch," Mackay says. The best forecasts available are predicting that this year's college graduates will have 10 job changes during their working lives. By the year 2000, new graduates can expect five *career* changes during their lives.

"The age of the specialist is over," Mackay says. Since job security is a thing of the past, the thing to work on is employability security. To position yourself so that you'll always be able to find work, you must be a generalist and you must keep learning, all your life.

Mackay's do list for job seekers is a bit different from some you may have seen. It goes beyond sending out a zillion copies of your perfect résumé, dressing for success, and firing off a thank-you note after the interview. Most of his recommendations apply equally to people who have jobs. They are habits for anyone to cultivate who wants to remain employable. Here are a few of the basics:

- *Set a routine for yourself and stick to it.* When you're looking for a job, the worst thing you can do is sleep late, slop around the house in your bathrobe and feel sorry for yourself. Write down your goals for the week and spend your hours working on them. A seemingly casual but potentially devastating question interviewers often ask is, "So, what have you done today?"

- *Get back in shape.*
- *Read.* Your local paper and *The Wall Street Journal* are musts. Books and periodicals in your field should be on your list, too. Mackay himself spends 35 hours a week reading.
- *Keep track.* Whether you use a Rolodex or a contact management computer program, keep notes on every person you meet—how and where you met them, and what you learned about them. Make this a habit you continue after you get a job, and for the rest of your life.

No matter what field or what stage of life you are in, your contacts are one of your most valuable assets to any potential employer. Mackay gives the example of his college-student daughter who desperately wanted to be a hostess at the campus's favorite beer joint. She was one of 137 applicants for the job. He asked her to think of what she had to offer that the others didn't. What she had were her lists of 45 students in her dance class, 95 women in her sorority, and 120 men in her boyfriend's fraternity. She promised the manager she would personally contact every one of those 260 people and ask them to come and see her at her new job. She got the job and delivered the bodies.

- *Volunteer.* Besides providing service to your community and being good for your soul, volunteering will keep you active, improve your job skills, and put you in contact with the most influential people in your community. "Volunteerism has changed my life," Mackay says. "Volunteering teaches you to be a leader, and is the single most important thing you can do to build a network. It's not a matter of joining a bunch of organizations and collecting business cards, but of finding creative ways of keeping in touch with people."

- *Don't confuse efforts with results.* Whether you're working to find a job or keep a job, Mackay believes it is vitally important not to confuse effort with results. A sharp interviewer is not impressed with how many activities you engaged in, but what you accomplished. The employer

 111

who is forced to cut staff won't be looking at how many hours you worked or how much sweat dripped from your brow, but how much business you brought through the door.

- *Expect rejections.* If at first you don't succeed, you're doing about par for the course today. Rejections can be expected and don't mean that you aren't qualified and didn't deserve the job, Mackay says. Everyone experiences setbacks and failures; it's how you react to them that makes a difference.

Too many people spin their wheels by "perfecting errors," Mackay thinks. "Practice makes perfect—NOT!" he says. "Perfect practice makes perfect."

If you are consistently getting "no" for an answer, it makes sense to analyze what you are doing right and what you are doing wrong. In job hunting, one of the commonest errors is thinking that "one size fits all." Your résumé must be customized for each job you apply for, and your preparation for each interview should be thoroughly customized.

"All someone would have to do to get a job at Mackay Envelope would be to prepare to win." Mackay says. A new graduate without career experience, for example, could ask for a plant tour at one of the company's competitors, talk to someone who sells envelopes, talk to a bulk mail house about differences in envelopes, and ask the Envelope Manufacturers of America to send him or her copies of the trade publications and information about issues affecting the industry. Then the job applicant could write to Mackay, ask for an interview, and mention a little of what he or she has learned in these investigations.

"Of the 500 people I've personally interviewed, only one has done that," Mackay says. Needless to say, the young man got a job with the company.

SUMMARY

It is important to remember that what you do after the interview can be almost as important as what you did in the actual interview. Follow-up activities will keep your name and application foremost in the employer's mind, and an in-depth self-evaluation will provide excellent preparation for future employment interviews. The circumstances of your job interview will determine what follow-up activities need to be accomplished.

The thank-you letter is an important follow-up activity. This formal letter shows your appreciation to the employer for granting you an interview. The letter should be sent two or three days after the interview, and it should use the professional techniques found in all good business letters.

If you decide you are not interested in the job after your interview, it is still a good idea to send a thank-you letter. This action preserves your reputation if you want to apply for another job with this organization in the future, or in case your name is mentioned by one employer to another for a particular position.

When an employer offers you a job, you should send a letter immediately acknowledging the job offer. Your objective is to thank the employer for the offer and tell him or her when you will give a decision on accepting the job.

A letter of acceptance should be sent as soon as you decide the job is for you. This is an exciting letter to write, and it should show your enthusiasm for starting a new job.

If you decide a particular job offer is not in your best interests, you should send a letter declining the offer. Compliment the employer about your interview, thank the interviewers, and give a reason why your declined the position. This action will again keep future options open.

It is common practice to follow up an interview with a telephone call. Always try to speak to one of the persons who interviewed you. Let them know you are still interested in the job, and ask when you can expect a decision. This call assures the employer of your continued interest in the organization.

When you live close to an employer, or when you know the employer personally, it is appropriate and recommended that you revisit the employer after the interview. Like the telephone follow-up, the visit demonstrates your continued interest in the position.

QUESTIONS FOR REVIEW AND DISCUSSION

1. Why is it always an important step in the job-seeking process to conduct after the interview follow-up activities?

   _____

   _____

   _____

2. What is the purpose of doing a conscientious self-evaluation of your just completed job interview?

   _____

   _____

   _____

3. What are some major reasons for sending a thank-you letter after an interview?

   _____

   _____

   _____

4. Why is it important to send a thank-you letter immediately after each interview?

   _____

   _____

   _____

5. What are your objectives in the first paragraph of a thank-you letter? Second paragraph? Third paragraph?

   _____

   _____

   _____

6. Why should you spend time writing a thank-you letter if you are no longer interested in the job?

   _____

   _____

   _____

7. What should you do if a company sends you a job offer and gives you two weeks to make a decision?

_____

_____

_____

8. In addition to saying yes, what other content should be included in a letter accepting a job offer?

_____

_____

_____

9. When you write a letter declining a job offer, why is it a good idea to compliment the employer on some phase of the job interview?

_____

_____

_____

10. Why is it a good idea to do a telephone follow-up call after a job interview?

_____

_____

_____

11. What should you say to the employer during a telephone follow-up call?

_____

_____

_____

12. When is it appropriate to revisit an employer after a job interview?

_____

_____

_____

13. What after-interview follow-up activities are absolutely necessary to help you get a job offer? Why?

_____

_____

_____

CASE STUDY

Julie Schwartz is one of your best friends. She recently interviewed for a sales position with Ross Formal Wear, and today received a letter asking her to come in for a second interview. Julie has some problems with the date and time for the interview, and she also knows she could use some help with the acceptance letter she has composed. Julie asks you to evaluate the letter and make any necessary corrections. Use a colored pen to correct the letter in Figure 6.10. Then determine at least one good suggestion to help Julie improve her future letter-writing activities. Add this suggestion to page 116.

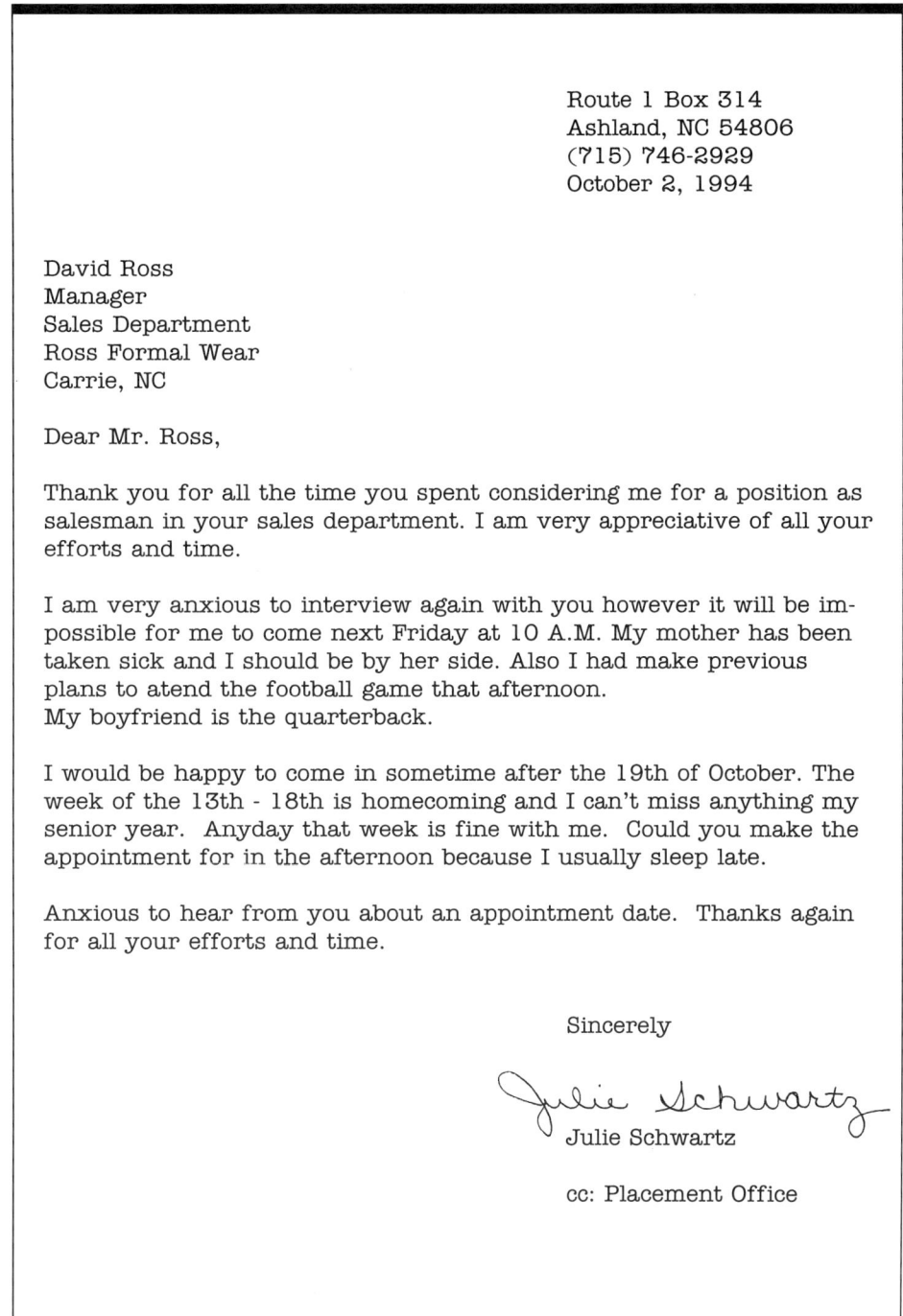

Route 1 Box 314
Ashland, NC 54806
(715) 746-2929
October 2, 1994

David Ross
Manager
Sales Department
Ross Formal Wear
Carrie, NC

Dear Mr. Ross,

Thank you for all the time you spent considering me for a position as salesman in your sales department. I am very appreciative of all your efforts and time.

I am very anxious to interview again with you however it will be impossible for me to come next Friday at 10 A.M. My mother has been taken sick and I should be by her side. Also I had make previous plans to atend the football game that afternoon.
My boyfriend is the quarterback.

I would be happy to come in sometime after the 19th of October. The week of the 13th - 18th is homecoming and I can't miss anything my senior year. Anyday that week is fine with me. Could you make the appointment for in the afternoon because I usually sleep late.

Anxious to hear from you about an appointment date. Thanks again for all your efforts and time.

Sincerely

Julie Schwartz
Julie Schwartz

cc: Placement Office

Figure 6-10. Julie Schwartz's Acceptance Letter

Now write a three-paragraph interview thank-you letter reminding the employer that you are still interested in the position. Use the same address and information that you used in the project on the previous page. Use all the thank-you letter principles in this chapter to write an outstanding letter that will keep you favorable in the employer's mind.

_____

_____

_____

_____

_____

_____

_____

_____

_____

_____

_____

_____

_____

_____

_____

_____

_____

_____

_____

_____

_____

_____

_____

_____

_____

_____

_____

_____

_____

_____

_____

_____

Your First Day and Month on the Job

After completing this chapter, you should be able to:

1. Develop habits that will help you prepare for the first day on the job, such as dressing appropriately, being punctual, remembering and organizing facts, knowing forms, and remembering names.

2. Meet employer expectations by using successful techniques in time management, customer service, listening, teaming, and wellness.

3. Identify additional skills that meet employer expectations.

4. Identify the categories that employers use to evaluate employees.

YOUR FIRST DAY

After your first day on the job, you may say: "I was never so overwhelmed in my life. There is so much to learn." Or you might say: "I don't have a real good handle on what my job description is. I hope someone gives me some direction." We hope you will say: "Wow, my first day was fantastic! The people I work with were so nice and helpful. I am really going to like working here." Whatever your reaction will be, this chapter should help you to succeed in your first days and months on the job.

Tomorrow you will be starting a fabulous new job. All of your job hunting skills are behind you and your new challenge is JOB SUCCESS. In your mind you will be asking yourself: "What will the first day be like? What should I wear? What are the people like that I am going to work with? What problems will I encounter?" Here are some suggestions to help you prepare for your first day.

DRESS APPROPRIATELY

If you have not investigated the proper attire for your new job, make sure you contact your employer and ask the question. The major goal of new employees on the first day of a new job is to make a good impression. Try not to "underdress" or "overdress." Ask a friend, spouse, or relative for advice. Wear clothing that is appropriate to the job you will be doing. Some colors, styles, and designs may be suitable for other environments but not the workplace. Obviously, good personal hygiene is a must. The bottom line on dressing appropriately is to dress as if you were going to a job interview. Supply yourself with the following job emergency kit:

- Breath mints or spray

- Safety pins

- Comb or brush

- Facial tissue

- Saline solution (if you wear contacts)

- Other needed personal hygiene items

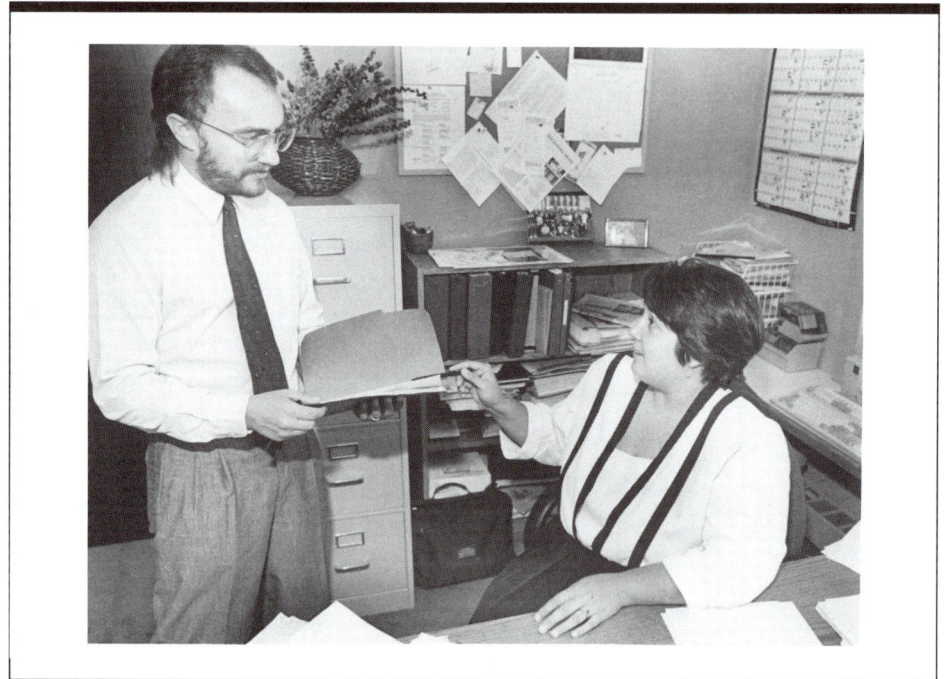

Make sure that your work clothing fits the needs of the job. Dressing appropriately can be the difference between making a good impression or a bad impression on your employer and fellow employees. (Photo by Mary Langenfeld.)

BE PUNCTUAL

A manager of a bank once stated that one of his best employees was a loan officer who was always five to ten minutes early for the job and always left five to ten minutes later than the job required. Take precautions, especially on your first day, to ensure you are not late. Remember too that punctuality also applies to breaks and lunch. Do not fall into a trap by listening to this statement: "Don't worry—no one is keeping track of break time or lunch time. Take as much time as you like."

USE A WRITING TABLET

Use a writing tablet (any color will do) to jot down names, special directions, locations, etc. that you will need to remember. The tablet is also a good method of keeping track of any questions you may have about the job. Most employers are impressed with employees who give the impression that they are organized. Many companies hold *orientation sessions* for new employees. These sessions will help you learn the mission, goals, policies, procedures, and operations of the company. Your tablet can be used to jot down important information obtained from these sessions.

KNOW AND COLLECT FORMS

Practically every business and industry uses forms for almost everything. The first forms you will be asked to fill out will probably be Federal Tax and State Tax withholding forms, as shown in Figure 7.1. This form, known as the W-4 form, will ask you how many dependents you claim. If you claim zero dependents, you will likely get some of your tax money back when you file your income tax. If you claim one or more dependents, you will receive more money each pay

1993 Form W-4 — Department of the Treasury, Internal Revenue Service

Purpose. Complete Form W-4 so that your employer can withhold the correct amount of Federal income tax from your pay.

Exemption From Withholding. Read line 7 of the certificate below to see if you can claim exempt status. *If exempt, complete line 7; but do not complete lines 5 and 6.* No Federal income tax will be withheld from your pay. Your exemption is good for one year only. It expires February 15, 1994.

Basic Instructions. Employees who are not exempt should complete the Personal Allowances Worksheet. Additional worksheets are provided on page 2 for employees to adjust their withholding allowances based on itemized deductions, adjustments to income, or two-earner/two-job situations. Complete all worksheets that apply to your situation. The worksheets will help you figure the number of withholding allowances you are entitled to claim. However, you may claim fewer allowances than this.

Head of Household. Generally, you may claim head of household filing status on your tax return only if you are unmarried and pay more than 50% of the costs of keeping up a home for yourself and your dependent(s) or other qualifying individuals.

Nonwage Income. If you have a large amount of nonwage income, such as interest or dividends, you should consider making estimated tax payments using Form 1040-ES. Otherwise, you may find that you owe additional tax at the end of the year.

Two-Earner/Two-Jobs. If you have a working spouse or more than one job, figure the total number of allowances you are entitled to claim on all jobs using worksheets from only one Form W-4. This total should be divided among all jobs. Your withholding will usually be most accurate when all allowances are claimed on the W-4 filed for the highest paying job and zero allowances are claimed for the others.

Advance Earned Income Credit. If you are eligible for this credit, you can receive it added to your paycheck throughout the year. For details, get Form W-5 from your employer.

Check Your Withholding. After your W-4 takes effect, you can use **Pub. 919,** Is My Withholding Correct for 1993?, to see how the dollar amount you are having withheld compares to your estimated total annual tax. Call 1-800-829-3676 to order this publication. Check your local telephone directory for the IRS assistance number if you need further help.

Personal Allowances Worksheet For 1993, the value of your personal exemption(s) is reduced if your income is over $108,450 ($162,700 if married filing jointly, $135,600 if head of household, or $81,350 if married filing separately). Get Pub. 919 for details.

A Enter "1" for **yourself** if no one else can claim you as a dependent . . . . A ______

B Enter "1" if:
- You are single and have only one job; or
- You are married, have only one job, and your spouse does not work; or
- Your wages from a second job or your spouse's wages (or the total of both) are $1,000 or less.

. . . B ______

C Enter "1" for your **spouse.** But, you may choose to enter -0- if you are married and have either a working spouse or more than one job (this may help you avoid having too little tax withheld) . . . . C ______

D Enter number of **dependents** (other than your spouse or yourself) whom you will claim on your tax return . . . . D ______

E Enter "1" if you will file as **head of household** on your tax return (see conditions under **Head of Household,** above) . E ______

F Enter "1" if you have at least $1,500 of **child or dependent care expenses** for which you plan to claim a credit . . F ______

G Add lines A through F and enter total here. **Note:** *This amount may be different from the number of exemptions you claim on your return* ▶ G ______

For accuracy, do all worksheets that apply.
- If you plan to **itemize or claim adjustments to income** and want to reduce your withholding, see the Deductions and Adjustments Worksheet on page 2.
- If you are **single** and have **more than one job** and your combined earnings from all jobs exceed $30,000 OR if you are **married** and have a **working spouse or more than one job,** and the combined earnings from all jobs exceed $50,000, see the Two-Earner/Two-Job Worksheet on page 2 if you want to avoid having too little tax withheld.
- If **neither** of the above situations applies, **stop here** and enter the number from line G on line 5 of Form W-4 below.

---------- **Cut here and give the certificate to your employer. Keep the top portion for your records.** ----------

Form **W-4** — Department of the Treasury, Internal Revenue Service

Employee's Withholding Allowance Certificate

▶ **For Privacy Act and Paperwork Reduction Act Notice, see reverse.**

OMB No. 1545-0010 — **1993**

1 Type or print your first name and middle initial | Last name | 2 Your social security number

Home address (number and street or rural route) | 3 ☐ Single ☐ Married ☐ Married, but withhold at higher Single rate.
Note: *If married, but legally separated, or spouse is a nonresident alien, check the Single box.*

City or town, state, and ZIP code | 4 If your last name differs from that on your social security card, check here and call 1-800-772-1213 for more information . . . . ▶ ☐

5 Total number of allowances you are claiming (from line G above or from the worksheets on page 2 if they apply) . | 5 |

6 Additional amount, if any, you want withheld from each paycheck . . . . | 6 | $

7 I claim exemption from withholding for 1993 and I certify that I meet **ALL** of the following conditions for exemption:
- Last year I had a right to a refund of **ALL** Federal income tax withheld because I had **NO** tax liability; **AND**
- This year I expect a refund of **ALL** Federal income tax withheld because I expect to have **NO** tax liability; **AND**
- This year if my income exceeds $600 and includes nonwage income, another person cannot claim me as a dependent.

If you meet all of the above conditions, enter "EXEMPT" here . . . . ▶ | 7 |

Under penalties of perjury, I certify that I am entitled to the number of withholding allowances claimed on this certificate or entitled to claim exempt status.

Employee's signature ▶ **Date ▶** , 19

8 Employer's name and address (Employer: Complete 8 and 10 only if sending to the IRS) | 9 Office code (optional) | 10 Employer identification number

Cat. No. 10220Q

Figure 7-1. W-4 Form, Page One

period and pay less taxes. However, in this case you may have to pay more taxes when you file and, depending upon your deductions, receive no money back from the federal or state government.

Page **2**

Deductions and Adjustments Worksheet

Note: *Use this worksheet only if you plan to itemize deductions or claim adjustments to income on your 1993 tax return.*

1	Enter an estimate of your 1993 itemized deductions. These include: qualifying home mortgage interest, charitable contributions, state and local taxes (but not sales taxes), medical expenses in excess of 7.5% of your income, and miscellaneous deductions. (For 1993, you may have to reduce your itemized deductions if your income is over $108,450 ($54,225 if married filing separately). Get Pub. 919 for details.)	1	$
2	Enter: { $6,200 if married filing jointly or qualifying widow(er) / $5,450 if head of household / $3,700 if single / $3,100 if married filing separately }	2	$
3	**Subtract** line 2 from line 1. If line 2 is greater than line 1, enter -0-	3	$
4	Enter an estimate of your 1993 adjustments to income. These include alimony paid and deductible IRA contributions	4	$
5	**Add** lines 3 and 4 and enter the total	5	$
6	Enter an estimate of your 1993 nonwage income (such as dividends or interest income)	6	$
7	**Subtract** line 6 from line 5. Enter the result, but not less than -0-	7	$
8	**Divide** the amount on line 7 by $2,500 and enter the result here. Drop any fraction	8	
9	Enter the number from Personal Allowances Worksheet, line G, on page 1	9	
10	**Add** lines 8 and 9 and enter the total here. If you plan to use the Two-Earner/Two-Job Worksheet, also enter the total on line 1, below. Otherwise, **stop here** and enter this total on Form W-4, line 5, on page 1.	10	

Two-Earner/Two-Job Worksheet

Note: *Use this worksheet only if the instructions for line G on page 1 direct you here.*

1	Enter the number from line G on page 1 (or from line 10 above if you used the Deductions and Adjustments Worksheet)	1	
2	Find the number in **Table 1** below that applies to the **LOWEST** paying job and enter it here	2	
3	If line 1 is **GREATER THAN OR EQUAL TO** line 2, subtract line 2 from line 1. Enter the result here (if zero, enter -0-) and on Form W-4, line 5, on page 1. **DO NOT** use the rest of this worksheet	3	

Note: *If line 1 is **LESS THAN** line 2, enter -0- on Form W-4, line 5, on page 1. Complete lines 4–9 to calculate the additional withholding amount necessary to avoid a year-end tax bill.*

4	Enter the number from line 2 of this worksheet	4	
5	Enter the number from line 1 of this worksheet	5	
6	**Subtract** line 5 from line 4	6	
7	Find the amount in **Table 2** below that applies to the **HIGHEST** paying job and enter it here	7	$
8	**Multiply** line 7 by line 6 and enter the result here. This is the additional annual withholding amount needed	8	$
9	Divide line 8 by the number of pay periods remaining in 1993. (For example, divide by 26 if you are paid every other week and you complete this form in December 1992.) Enter the result here and on Form W-4, line 6, page 1. This is the additional amount to be withheld from each paycheck	9	$

Table 1: Two-Earner/Two-Job Worksheet

Married Filing Jointly		All Others	
If wages from **LOWEST** paying job are—	Enter on line 2 above	If wages from **LOWEST** paying job are—	Enter on line 2 above
0 - $3,000	0	0 - $6,000	0
3,001 - 8,000	1	6,001 - 11,000	1
8,001 - 13,000	2	11,001 - 15,000	2
13,001 - 18,000	3	15,001 - 19,000	3
18,001 - 22,000	4	19,001 - 24,000	4
22,001 - 27,000	5	24,001 - 50,000	5
27,001 - 31,000	6	50,001 and over	6
31,001 - 35,000	7		
35,001 - 40,000	8		
40,001 - 60,000	9		
60,001 - 85,000	10		
85,001 and over	11		

Table 2: Two-Earner/Two-Job Worksheet

Married Filing Jointly		All Others	
If wages from **HIGHEST** paying job are—	Enter on line 7 above	If wages from **HIGHEST** paying job are—	Enter on line 7 above
0 - $ 50,000	$350	0 - $30,000	$350
50,001 - 100,000	660	30,001 - 60,000	660
100,001 and over	730	60,001 and over	730

Privacy Act and Paperwork Reduction Act Notice.—We ask for the information on this form to carry out the Internal Revenue laws of the United States. The Internal Revenue Code requires this information under sections 3402(f)(2)(A) and 6109 and their regulations. Failure to provide a completed form will result in your being treated as a single person who claims no withholding allowances. Routine uses of this information include giving it to the Department of Justice for civil and criminal litigation and to cities, states, and the District of Columbia for use in administering their tax laws.

The time needed to complete this form will vary depending on individual circumstances. The estimated average time is: **Recordkeeping** 46 min., **Learning about the law or the form** 10 min., **Preparing the form** 69 min. If you have comments concerning the accuracy of these time estimates or suggestions for making this form more simple, we would be happy to hear from you. You can write to both the **Internal Revenue Service,** Washington, DC 20224, Attention: IRS Reports Clearance Officer, T:FP; and the **Office of Management and Budget,** Paperwork Reduction Project (1545-0010), Washington, DC 20503. **DO NOT** send the tax form to either of these offices. Instead, give it to your employer.

☆ **U.S. GOVERNMENT PRINTING OFFICE:** 1993 315-082

Figure 7-1. W-4 Form, Page Two

Another form you may be required to fill out will be an Employment Eligibility Verification form, known as the I-9 form. This form, shown in Figure 7.2, is required by the United States Department of Justice and is a means to prove who you really are. Under penalty of perjury, you must declare to be a citizen of the United States or a lawful or authorized alien.

In addition, you will need to provide two other documents to prove your identity and employment eligibility to the employer. Figure 7.3 indicates a list of acceptable documents approved by the Justice Department and the Bureau of Immigration and Naturalization Services. If you are a natural citizen of the

U.S. Department of Justice
Immigration and Naturalization Service

OMB No. 1115-0136
Employment Eligibility Verification

Please read instructions carefully before completing this form. The instructions must be available during completion of this form. ANTI-DISCRIMINATION NOTICE. It is illegal to discriminate against work eligible individuals. Employers CANNOT specify which document(s) they will accept from an employee. The refusal to hire an individual because of a future expiration date may also constitute illegal discrimination.

Section 1. Employee Information and Verification. To be completed and signed by employee at the time employment begins

| Print Name: Last | First | Middle Initial | Maiden Name |

| Address (Street Name and Number) | Apt. # | Date of Birth (month/day/year) |

| City | State | Zip Code | Social Security # |

I am aware that federal law provides for imprisonment and/or fines for false statements or use of false documents in connection with the completion of this form.

I attest, under penalty of perjury, that I am (check one of the following):
☐ A citizen or national of the United States
☐ A Lawful Permanent Resident (Alien # A _____)
☐ An alien authorized to work until ___/___/___
(Alien # or Admission # _____)

| Employee's Signature | Date (month/day/year) |

Preparer and/or Translator Certification. (To be completed and signed if Section 1 is prepared by a person other than the employee.) I attest, under penalty of perjury, that I have assisted in the completion of this form and that to the best of my knowledge the information is true and correct.

| Preparer's/Translator's Signature | Print Name |

| Address (Street Name and Number, City, State, Zip Code) | Date (month/day/year) |

Section 2. Employer Review and Verification. To be completed and signed by employer. Examine one document from List A OR examine one document from List B and one from List C as listed on the reverse of this form and record the title, number and expiration date, if any, of the document(s)

	List A	OR	List B	AND	List C
Document title:					
Issuing authority:					
Document #:					
Expiration Date (if any):	___/___/___		___/___/___		___/___/___
Document #:					
Expiration Date (if any):	___/___/___				

CERTIFICATION - I attest, under penalty of perjury, that I have examined the document(s) presented by the above-named employee, that the above-listed document(s) appear to be genuine and to relate to the employee named, that the employee began employment on (month/day/year) ___/___/___ and that to the best of my knowledge the employee is eligible to work in the United States. (State employment agencies may omit the date the employee began employment).

| Signature of Employer or Authorized Representative | Print Name | Title |

| Business or Organization Name | Address (Street Name and Number, City, State, Zip Code) | Date (month/day/year) |

Section 3. Updating and Reverification. To be completed and signed by employer

| A. New Name (if applicable) | B. Date of rehire (month/day/year) (if applicable) |

C. If employee's previous grant of work authorization has expired, provide the information below for the document that establishes current employment eligibility.

Document Title: _____ Document #: _____ Expiration Date (if any): ___/___/___

I attest, under penalty of perjury, that to the best of my knowledge, this employee is eligible to work in the United States, and if the employee presented document(s), the document(s) I have examined appear to be genuine and to relate to the individual.

| Signature of Employer or Authorized Representative | Date (month/day/year) |

Form I-9 (Rev. 11-21-91) N

Figure 7-2. U.S. Department of Justice Form I-9

United States, you will need one document from LIST A and one document from LIST B only.

The following are the usual types of forms used by businesses:

- **Absence or sick leave.** This form is used by the employer if the employee is absent due to sickness or other reasons.

- **Payroll deduction form.** On this form, you allow your employer to withhold some of your net income and transfer it to a savings account, checking account, or special fund like United Way or other charitable fund.

- **Travel and meeting expenses form.** Usually, employers will reimburse you for company travel, food, lodging expenses and meeting expenses. These type of expenses are reported on a form like the one shown in Figure 7.4.

LISTS OF ACCEPTABLE DOCUMENTS

LIST A	OR	LIST B	AND	LIST C
Documents that Establish Both Identity and Employment Eligibility		**Documents that Establish Identity**		**Documents that Establish Employment Eligibility**

LIST A	LIST B	LIST C
1. U.S. Passport (unexpired or expired)	1. Driver's license or ID card issued by a state or outlying possession of the United States provided it contains a photograph or information such as name, date of birth, sex, height, eye color, and address	1. U.S. social security card issued by the Social Security Administration (*other than a card stating it is not valid for employment*)
2. Certificate of U.S. Citizenship (*INS Form N-560 or N-561*)		
3. Certificate of Naturalization (*INS Form N-550 or N-570*)	2. ID card issued by federal, state, or local government agencies or entities provided it contains a photograph or information such as name, date of birth, sex, height, eye color, and address	2. Certification of Birth Abroad issued by the Department of State (*Form FS-545 or From DS-1350*)
4. Unexpired foreign passport, with *I-551 stamp* or attached *INS Form I-94* indicating unexpired employment authorization	3. School ID card with a photograph	3. Original or certified copy of a birth certificate issued by a state, county, municipal authority or outlying possession of the United States bearing an official seal
5. Alien Registration Receipt Card with photograph (*INS Form I-151 or I-551*)	4. Voter's registration card	
6. Unexpired Temporary ResidentCard (*INS Form I-688*)	5. U.S. Military card or draft record	
	6. Military dependent's ID card	4. Native American tribal document
7. Unexpired Employment Authorization Card (*INS Form I-688A*)	7. U.S. Coast Guard Merchant Mariner Card	
	8. Native American tribal document	5. U.S. Citizen ID Card (*INS Form I-197*)
8. Unexpired Reentry Permit (*INSForm I-327*)	9. Driver's license issued by a Canadian government authority	
9. Unexpired Refugee Travel Document (*INS Form I-571*)	**For persons under age 18 who are unable to present a document listed above:**	6. ID Card for use of Resident Citizen in the United States (*INS Form I-179*)
10. Unexpired Employment Authorization Document issued by the INS which contains a photograph (*INS Form I-688B*)	10. School record or report card	7. Unexpired employment authorization document issued by the INS (*other than those listed under List A*)
	11. Clinic, doctor, or hospital record	
	12. Day-care or nursery school record	

Illustrations of many of these documents appear in Part 8 of the Handbook for Employers (M-274)

Form I-9 (Rev. 11-21-91) N

Figure 7-3. List of Acceptable Documents

- **Supplies form.** If you need to requisition paper supplies, pens, computer disks, printer ribbons, and other consumable supplies, you would use a supplies form.

- **Equipment.** Usually an equipment form is used to requisition equipment that is budgeted by your company for your use.

- **Maintenance or repair form.** If the above equipment breaks down, you may need a form to requisition the repair of equipment. The form is also used to maintain service on a piece of equipment like a computer, copier, or fax machine.

- **Room or facility usage form.** You may also need to fill out a room or facility usage form if you need a room for a meeting or conference.

- **Coffee fund form.** In some companies, coffee and other beverages are a shared expense, and this form is used to keep track of who are paying their share.

- **Inter-departmental communications form.** On this form, you would communicate messages or correspondence to others within your company. Many companies are replacing this form with computerized messages called *e mail,* or electronic mail.

REMEMBER NAMES

Have you ever heard someone say, "I sure have a hard time remembering names"? Psychologists tell us that people in general love to hear their name when addressed. If you do not practice this skill, remembering names can be difficult. Here are a few suggestions to help you:

1. Listen carefully and repeat the person's name when introduced.

2. Associate the person's name with something unique about that person. For example: Mark has no hair; Yolanda wears gold jewelry; Jon is very tall.

3. Associate the person's name with what they do or with what department they work in. For example: Iris in accounting; Theresa in computers.

4. As mentioned previously, jot down the person's name on a tablet for future reference.

5. If you missed a name or cannot remember a name, reintroduce yourself and use the methods above.

YOUR FIRST MONTH

For the first few weeks on the job you were expected to be a little ignorant about the way things work. But now you should be getting a handle on company operations and procedures. Whether you are using this job as a building block for career development, or this job is what you plan to do the rest of your life, you need to be aware of what successful traits your employer is looking for. Remember this Golden Rule: EMPLOYERS WANT EMPLOYEES WITH GOOD COMMUNICATION AND INTERPERSONAL HUMAN RELATIONS SKILLS. More than anything else, these skills contribute to the success of the business or industry. The following suggestions will help you develop some of these skills:

LISTEN CAREFULLY

In business and industry, workers, supervisors, managers, and employees at all levels may be required to share ideas as well as follow instructions. Employees who

```
                              EXPENSE REPORT


DATES: _____     CITY: _____


PURPOSE OF TRIP: _____
      _____
      _____
      _____


TRANSPORTATION:      HOSPITAL CAR: _____

                     PERSONAL VEHICLE _____ MILES @   ¢/MILE   $ _____

                     AIR ...........(vendor)...................................................$ _____

                     OTHER ...............................................................$ _____




LODGING: .................HOTEL/MOTEL ...........(INCLUDE ITEMIZED BILL) ................$ _____

MEALS: ...................INCLUDE ITEMIZED BILLS OR RECEIPTS ..........................$ _____

OTHER: .....................................................................................$ _____

MISCELLANEOUS:  EXPLAIN AND INCLUDE RECEIPTS .................................$ _____

                                         SUB-TOTAL .......................$ _____
                                         LESS CASH ADVANCE........$ _____

                                         TOTAL................................$ _____


REPORT SUBMITTED BY:           Name _____
                               Address _____
                                       _____


DEPARTMENT HEAD APPROVAL _____ (SIGNATURE)
                      DATE _____


RETURN TO THE ACCOUNTING DEPARTMENT. NO TUITION CHECKS, MEALS, TRANSPORTATION,
                      ETC. WILL BE ISSUED UNTIL FORM IS COMPLETE.
                      PLEASE ALLOW 2 WEEKS FOR PROCESSING.

          _____

ACCOUNTS PAYABLE DEPARTMENT: _____ _____

                      EXPENSE ACCOUNT DISTRIBUTION_____
```

Figure 7-4. Expense Account Form

need to succeed at such interpersonal skills will do well to improve their listening skills. The following six "listening rules" should help:

1. Use good eye contact when listening to someone. If your eyes wander from the speaker, your mind will follow and cause you to miss important information.

2. When you do not understand the speaker, ask questions or ask the speaker to repeat or explain.

3. Do not interrupt the speaker. Wait until the person is done talking. Remember that you cannot talk and listen at the same time.

4. Watch out for emotional or sensitive words. These words distract you from listening to the speaker. Example: race, gender, political, religious, social, etc.

5. Concentrate on the speaker's message and not on the speaker. In our subconscious, we may be judging what people say by their looks.

6. Do not let your mind wander. Good concentration will help you to overcome the tendency to wander.

BE A TEAM PLAYER

To improve product quality and give employees decision-making abilities, Japanese manufacturers took advantage of a new management technique called *Total Quality Management*. They developed "quality circles" composed of teams of employees, each responsible for the quality of an entire product. The TQM approach moves away from the notion that management should control all aspects of the work. In the new "quality culture," people of all skill levels work together to plan, organize, and implement projects. TQM is now becoming accepted in the United States as well. In the marketing department of the Exxon Company, for example, Total Quality Management is becoming increasingly used. Exxon emphasizes the importance of an employee's ability to work with others.

Be careful. Some firms have not implemented the TQM process or a team approach. You may want to suggest it. However, your firm may not be ready to implement TQM. It takes commitment and training. Remember that working as a good team player will usually bring success.

PRACTICE GOOD CUSTOMER SERVICE

Most companies, including Exxon, insist that employees treat customers as their most important commodity. Providing good customer service as an employee will reap many rewards in this competitive world. **Customer service** can be defined as treating the customers with respect, meeting their needs, and doing it in a friendly manner.

Your company may consider that the employees you work with, especially the employees who report to you, are also customers. Basically, the rules of good customer service apply to fellow employees. Here are the Ten Commandments of Customer Service:

1. TREAT others as if you were those others.

2. PRAISE others.

3. Be SINCERE.

4. USE A PERSON'S NAME when speaking to them.

5. BE A FRIEND.

6. SMILE.

7. LISTEN to others.

8. THINK YOU instead of I.

9. GIVE to others.

10. CARE for others.

AVOID OFFICE POLITICS

You may be tempted to take sides when disputes, decisions, cliques, and gossip are present. In most cases you will be better off to play neutral and avoid cases and situations that could jeopardize your employment. For example, you could be asked to take sides in a dispute between managers on job responsibilities. A question you can always ask is: "How could the problem or dispute be solved by compromise, where it can be a win—win situation?" Here are some suggestions to follow when office politics are apparent:

- **Keep from spreading gossip.** You may want to state that you have heard rumors, but you felt that it was none of you business.

- **Do not take sides in disputes.** Look for compromises or optional solutions. Always stick to the facts.

- **Watch out for cliques.** Associate with several employees on breaks or lunch hours.

EXPERT *Advice*
OFFICE POLITICS

Your peers may disdain you. And your personal integrity may take a beating. But your career could get a boost if you remember that the boss is always right. "Kissing up" works.

Excessive flattery, expressing attitudes similar to those held by a supervisor and making the most of opportunities to please the boss are the mainstays of workers trying to ingratiate themselves, say the experts. And even though everybody can see through those ploys—even the boss—the tactics work just the same.

They work because it is human nature to appreciate compliments, to want reassurance that your attitudes are correct, and to like the people who admire you. So even when the boss knows you are kissing up, it still pays off—literally—in positive job evaluations, promotions, and higher pay.

Everybody intuitively seems to know that kissing up works. This summer, however, two professors from Bryant College in Smithfield, Rhode Island, have released a study that measures just how well it works. According to their study, based on 1991 data, kissing up gives a worker a 4 percent to 5 percent advantage over someone who relies simply on job performance to achieve success.

"Performance is important; you've got to perform. But ingratiation does something more. It gives you an edge," said Ronald Deluga, an associate professor of psychology at Bryant College, who, with J. T. Perry, a management department instructor, conducted the research and co-authored the study.

For study purposes, methods of kissing up were divided into three categories:

- **Opinion uniformity:** agreeing with the boss.

- **Self-presentation:** acting the way the boss likes.

- **Other enhancement:** flattering the boss.

Although all three methods led to improved employee-supervisor relations, opinion uniformity (agreeing with the boss) was the most popularly used ingratiation method and the most effective, according to the survey.

Second in popularity and effectiveness was self-presentation (behaving in a way the supervisor will like).

The third category, other enhancement (flattery), was the least popular and was ranked least effective.

Fewer workers admitted using flattery and fewer supervisors admitted being susceptible to it, according to Deluga, "because it's a little obvious."

Although kissing up is widely practiced and generally rewarded, the study does note a downside. The tactic may benefit the practitioner, but it may not be in the best interest of the higher-up being flattered—or the company.
The ascendancy of "yes people" can undermine critical thinking and allow top managers to ignore problems, according to the study and area management consultants. Also, these days when team building is a popular method of getting work done, disingenuous ingratiation can cause tensions and distrust that hurt group efforts.

(Source: "KISSING UP TO BOSS WORKS, BUT THERE'S A DOWNSIDE," by Maida Odom, Knight-Rider News Service, August 14, 1993.)

PRACTICE TIME MANAGEMENT

Practice good time management. If you want to accomplish your short term and long term goals, then good time management is a must. Everyone would like an additional hour or two in every work day to get organized or to catch up. However, we wouldn't need this hour if we practiced good time management techniques in the first place. Let us look at ten of the leading time wasters:

1. Telephone interruptions

2. Visitors without appointments

3. Meetings that are unorganized

4. Crisis situations unplanned for

5. Cluttered desk and personal disorganization

6. Not delegating appropriately

7. Lack of objectives, priorities, and deadlines

8. Inability to say no

9. Inaccurate or inadequate information from others

10. Indecision and procrastination

When practicing good time management, there are some techniques that have proven successful. They include:

1. **Keep a pocket calendar or planner.** Some planners are very sophisticated and you will need instruction on how to use them. A monthly pocket calendar is the minimum time management tool you should use. It is easy to jot down your appointments, meetings, priorities, etc.

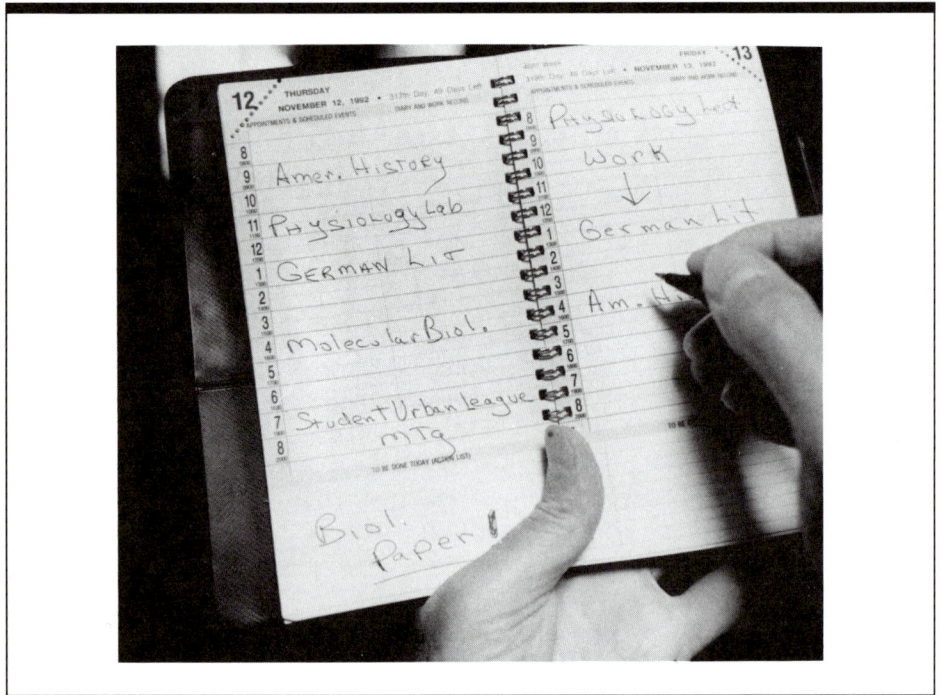

Practicing good time management is essential in the workplace. Using a pocket calendar or planner is an excellent way of keeping track of appointments, meetings, and priorities. (Photo by Mary Langenfeld.)

2. **Organize your work.** Develop an "A" stack for the papers you need to address. Then, develop a "B" stack for the papers that can be addressed after the "A" papers have been taken care of. Generally these are papers whose deadlines are not as immediate as the "A" papers. Finally develop a "C" stack for papers that you can address only if you have time. Try to handle all of these papers only once.

3. **Prioritize your work day.** Develop a "to do list." Write down on a small piece of paper all the things you need to accomplish on a given day. Prioritize what the important items are. Then, cross out the work tasks you have accomplished as you refer to your list throughout the day.

DEVELOP A WELLNESS APPROACH TO LIFE

Good health is the key to your emotional, physical, and intellectual well-being. More employers are developing programs that provide health maintenance to their employees. Not only will good health and wellness add to your job success, but your chances are greater that you will reach your potential. There are many community, health, and education programs available to help you become healthy. Here are some suggestions for developing a wellness approach to life:

1. **Practice good eating habits.** Avoid fats, drink water, count calories, take vitamins, and eat a balanced diet.

2. **Avoid drugs.** Stay away from tobacco, excessive alcohol, and illegal drugs.

3. **Exercise.** Participate in aerobic or recreational activities. Walking is recommended by many exercise experts.

4. **Rest.** Good sleeping habits are a must.

5. **Have a sense of humor.** Good humor is a great way to get a healthy outlook on life.

6. **Cope with stress.** Be positive. Focus on what you can control. Eliminate the cause of stress. Relieve the symptoms by practicing the above.

OTHER EMPLOYMENT SKILLS

As mentioned earlier in this chapter, once you are past the initial employment stage and are comfortable with your job, you need to implement skills that most employers expect employees to have in the 1990s. These skills include:

- Initiative

- Self-confidence

- Creativity

- Thinking with fresh ideas

- Good communication

- Ability to learn and change

- Positive working relationships

- Having a sense of humor

PERFORMANCE EVALUATION

During your orientation, your employer should identify the method the company uses to evaluate employees. In addition, the employer should communicate to you when evaluations will be done and who will be doing the evaluation. Generally speaking, it will be your immediate supervisor. Furthermore, your employer may want to let you know the categories your performance evaluation will be based on. These categories may include the following:

- **Quality of work.** Do you meet the standards of quality performance asked for by your employer?

- **Quantity of work.** Are you producing the amount of work expected by the employer?

- **Ability to learn.** Have you done a good job of learning the duties and responsibilities of your job description? Do you catch on to new technology?

- **Attitude.** Do you possess a good attitude about your company, your job, your co-workers, and your boss?

- **Cooperation.** Do you work well with other workers? Are you a team player?

- **Initiative.** Do you perform duties beyond what is called for by your employer? Do you look for additional tasks to perform when you have completed your required tasks?

- **Communications.** Do you communicate information appropriately to management, co-workers, and/or customers?

In addition to this list, you may be evaluated on other skills such as appearance, attendance, punctuality, organization, customer relations, resourcefulness, and leadership. In any case, remember that evaluations are used to measure commendable performance as well as areas that need improvement. Try to set your job goals based upon your evaluation. Continue to do what you do best and improve what needs to be improved.

SUMMARY

Your first days and months on the job are very important as you move down your career path. This chapter has given you some tools to succeed. On the first day, you must remember to:

- Dress appropriately

- Be punctual

- Use a writing tablet

- Know and collect forms

- Remember names

To meet employer expectations as your career progresses, remember that employers want employees with good communication and interpersonal human relations skills. These skills include:

- Listening carefully

- Being a team player

- Practicing good customer service

- Avoiding office politics

- Practicing time management

- Developing a wellness approach to life

In addition, employers may expect initiative, self-confidence, creativity, fresh ideas, good communication, ability to learn and change, and a positive work attitude.

Most employers will evaluate your job performance on a six-month or yearly basis. Be prepared to accept evaluations as a measurement for performing well or for identifying areas that need improvement or change.

Now you must implement the good employment techniques outlined in this chapter. Technology is changing rapidly, but most of the skills mentioned in this chapter will remain constant. Build upon your jobs, your successes, failures, experiences, and physical and mental health to land the job you will be most happy with. Good luck!

QUESTIONS FOR REVIEW AND DISCUSSION

1. Seymour Clutz has a history of forgetting things, being late, losing directions, and getting lost. This is Seymour's first day on his new job. What advice could you give Seymour to help him succeed?

_____

_____

_____

2. What are various ways a writing tablet can be used on the job?

_____

_____

_____

3. List the forms discussed in the chapter and determine why it is necessary to use each.

_____

_____

_____

4. Jon, Nicole, Howard, William, Carmen, Desmond, and Elena are employees you have just been introduced to on your job. How can you remember their names?

_____

_____

_____

5. Why do you think it is harder to listen than to talk?

_____

_____

_____

6. If you were to list rules for being a good team player, what would be included in your list?

_____

_____

_____

7. Do you think that students are "customers" of the teacher?

_____

_____

_____

8. What are your daily time wasters? Suggest ways that you can overcome them.

_____

_____

_____

9. Ima Wreck shows signs of fatigue, tiredness, and stress every day on the job. She asks for your help. What questions would you ask her and what suggestions might you give her?

_____

_____

_____

10. Develop a "to do" list for tomorrow's activities. How can you make sure it is going to be followed?

_____

_____

_____

CASE STUDY

You are a career counselor for the U.S. Career Corporation. One day, Ima Down calls to make an appointment with you to discuss her career as a real estate agent. She is having trouble adjusting to the regimen of being a real estate broker, and thinks she is in the wrong career even though she likes what she is doing. Ima says she is having a lot of problems. As her career counselor, what questions would you ask Ima when she comes in for her appointment? What would be your prescription if you found out that her problem was time management?

PROJECT

Interview several human resource managers and survey what types of employee training and development programs are taking place relative to quality, wellness, problem solving, team building, coaching, leadership, etc. Report to your instructor on what you have learned. This is a good team project.

CHAPTER 8

Work Ethics

After completing this chapter you should be able to:

1. Explain why ethics are important.

2. Develop the types of work ethics needed for job success.

3. Define sexual harassment.

4. Identify workplace situations that would be considered sexual harassment violations.

5. Develop procedures to confront harassment problems.

THE IMPORTANCE OF ETHICS

Getting a job through proper application procedures is half the battle. The other half is keeping your job. You want to use your job to build a career whether you stay with your current position or switch jobs. You want a reputation as a trusted employee, known for your honesty, sincerity, and good moral character. The last thing you want to happen is to be fired for not displaying proper ethical procedures.

DEFINING ETHICS

The Webster Dictionary defines **ethics** as "moral principles or codes of conduct." When referring to employment, ethics is a term associated with honesty, trust, legal behavior, and the decent treatment of others. Some companies have developed a "code of ethics" that employees are expected to follow (see EXPERT ADVICE).

EXPERT *Advice*

ONE COMPANY'S CODE OF ETHICS

(Editor's note: Terence E. Adderley is President and CEO of the Kelly Services Corporation, a national employment agency that deals mainly with the temporary placement of workers. Each employee of Kelly Services is given an Ethics Booklet to read and follow. The following is the first page of the booklet in which Mr. Adderley talks about ethics at Kelly Services.)

Dear Fellow Employee:

A corporation's reputation is built by, and on, its people. The opinion others have of Kelly is a result of the personal integrity and day-to-day performance of all the people who work for our company.

The hard work and high standards demonstrated by all Kelly employees for more than forty years have earned Kelly an outstanding reputation for ethical behavior and fair dealing.

In our business activities, we encounter a variety of ethical and legal questions. The way we resolve these issues should be consistent with Kelly's basic values and principles. We are committed to responsible corporate citizenship to the many communities in which we reside and to society as a whole. As a responsible corporate citizen it is Kelly's policy to comply with the law in the communities in which we operate.

This booklet describes our values and the ethical standards that Kelly employees follow in carrying out our day-to-day responsibilities.

The values and standards discussed in this booklet are intended to provide a general guideline of expectation. This is not a rule book. It makes no attempt to provide specific answers for every situation that you might encounter. Indeed, in most cases, your own personal integrity and good judgment must be the best guide to ethical and responsible conduct.

You will notice that there are no changes from Kelly's existing policies, practices, and procedures. Issuance of this guide simply reaffirms and expresses in writing Kelly's wholehearted and sincere commitment to the highest standards of business conduct.

Kelly's integrity and reputation are in your hands. I am confident you will continue to carry our outstanding reputation into the future.

Terence E. Adderley

Some ethical choices and problems are difficult to deal with, while others are relatively simple. Take, for example, the following story:

> Debra came home from school one day with a note from the high school principal reprimanding her for taking pens and paper from school that did not belong to her. Her mother said, "Wait until your father comes home. He is really going to be angry." So when Debra's dad got home he said, "I am disappointed in you, Debra; you know we expect your best behavior at school. If you needed paper and pens, why didn't you say something to me? I could have gotten you all the pens and paper you need at work!"

Sometimes we are brought up in an environment where ethics can be confusing. We think certain activities are okay because everyone does it. For example, if an employee takes ten minutes more than the time allotted for lunch, is it right because all employees do it? If an employee or manager writes down on an expense form more money than what was actually spent (known as "padding the account"), is it right because others pad their expense accounts? Or, as in the above example, is it okay for some people, but not okay for us? The father could take supplies from work, but did not want his daughter to do the same at her school. Thus, a double standard was created. Relating back to the definition of ethics, if it is wrong, then it is wrong for everyone.

ETHICAL ISSUES IN THE WORKPLACE

Some employer once said, "I want an honest day's work for an honest day's pay." This may be an over-simplified statement on ethics, but it certainly is true.

Employers' expectations regarding ethics are extremely high. In the workplace, there are many challenges to a worker's ethical behavior. Proper ethical behavior can lead to a successful and long-lasting relationship with an employer.

Figure 8.1 takes a look at some of the ethical issues that may confront us at work. This figure represents some of the more common ethical issues that employees may have to face while working. You may want to test yourself using Figure 8.2 to see if you have a good ethical philosophy.

ETHICAL ISSUES

Ethical Issue	What Not to Do/What to Do
1. Using sick days for vacation days	Sick days are for that purpose only. You cost the firm time and money when you are not at work. Use only sick days when needed—illness or immediate family illness.
2. Taking supplies for personal use	Supplies are not free. They cost the company money. Purchase your own supplies for personal use.
3. Padding an expense account	Do not add extra expenses on your expense account. Record the expenses you actually spent. Receipts are a good way to keep track.
4. Misrepresenting the product, service, or firm	Avoid giving false facts about a product or service. Honesty is always the best policy. Even if it means losing a sale, customers expect a company to have honest employees.
5. Conducting other business on company time	It is not proper to use company time to conduct your personal business or affairs. Conducting other business is a conflict of interest. You are paid for the time the company hired you for.
6. Hiring a relative or friend over someone else	Hiring a member of your immediate family or a close friend when another candidate is more qualified is not ethical. Always hire the best candidate based upon objective and affirmative criteria.
7. Copying or borrowing software	Do not copy any software without reading the licensing agreements. Any variation or creative use of software may be illegal.
8. Gossiping or giving out confidential information	If you are in doubt as to whether information is gossip or confidential, ask your boss. Avoid spreading information that is not backed up by proper and appropriate documentation.

Figure 8-1. Ethical Issues

ETHICAL ISSUES	
Ethical Issue	**What Not to Do/What to Do**
9. Favoritism or discrimination toward other employees	Be careful not to favor one employee over another when dealing with assignments and promotions. Always deal with other employees with fairness and objectivity.
10. Drugs or alcohol usage at work	This is absolutely not tolerated on the job. There are Alcohol and Drug Abuse (AODA) programs in many companies and communities to deal with this problem.

Figure 8-1. Ethical Issues (con'd)

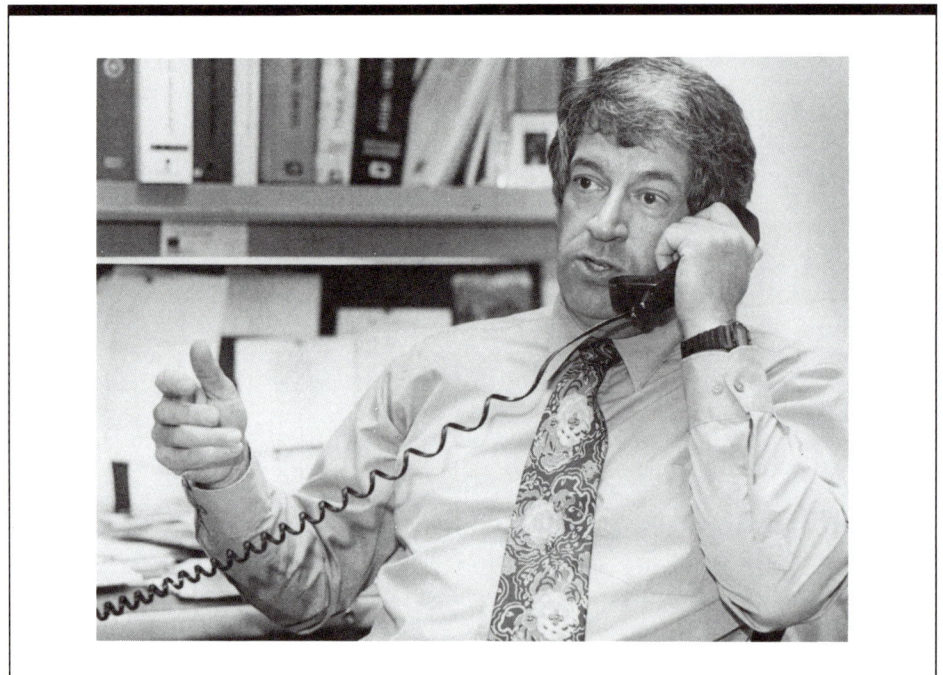

Keep your personal telephone conversations to an absolute minimum at work. Conducting personal business on company time may be seen as a conflict of interest or simply as a misuse of the telephone. (Photo by Mary Langenfeld.)

One of the most difficult problems regarding ethics in the 1990s concerns "sexual harassment." This issue will be discussed next.

SEXUAL HARASSMENT ON THE JOB

Policies regarding sexual harassment have existed in many companies for a long time. However, some of these policies were never enforced or followed, and in some cases, violations were swept under the carpet. Lawsuits and court cases began to bring this problem to light. Nothing has brought the issue of sexual harassment before the public eye more than the Thomas-Hill hearings in 1992.

Judge Clarence Thomas, prior to his Supreme Court appointment approval by the U.S. Senate, was accused by a former employee, Anita Hill, of sexual harassment. Obviously, this allegation attracted the attention of the media and, as a

TEST YOUR ETHICS

When you become employed in the 1990s, you will encounter every day situations that will test your ethical values and judgment. Ethical challenges are not always easy. At times, an ethical dilemma could put you in a "no-win" situation. The following test should give you an idea of what ethical decisions you may have to face someday at work. Do not expect to score too high. Good luck.

<u>Circle the number that best matches your opinion.</u>

Scoring:			
Strongly Disagree	=	4
Disagree	=	3
Agree	=	2
Strongly Agree	=	1

1) Employees should always do what their bosses suggest, even though it may not be the right thing to do.　　1　2　3　4

2) Expense accounts are sometimes difficult to keep accurate. Thus, it may be necessary to give approximate figures.　　1　2　3　4

3) Bringing home company pens, pencils, tape, etc., for personal use is an accepted fringe benefit.　　1　2　3　4

4) As employees you should not be expected to "squeal" on peers for their improper behavior.　　1　2　3　4

5) In the 1990s, it is sometimes necessary to conduct personal business on company time.　　1　2　3　4

6) It is good psychology to set goals above what is considered normal to obtain a greater effort from employees.　　1　2　3　4

7) It is acceptable to use company equipment, like a computer or copier, for community or personal use.　　1　2　3　4

8) At times it is proper to quote a "hopeful" shipping date to get the order.　　1　2　3　4

9) There are times when your employees can overlook contract and safety violations to get the job done.　　1　2　3　4

10) At times embarrassing work-related information can be withheld from your boss.　　1　2　3　4

11) Needed personal calls can be used on the company's long distance line.　　1　2　3　4

12) When receiving goods, overage need not be reported.　　1　2　3　4

13) There are always exceptions to company policies and procedures.　　1　2　3　4

SCORING:　　ADD UP ALL ANSWERS

52	= Super Ethical Values
46-51	= Excellent Ethics
40-45	= Good Ethics
35-39	= Average Ethics
30-34	= Need moral development
0-29	= Do you like prison?

Figure 8-2. Test Your Ethics

result of this hearing, employers began to revitalize, initiate, educate, and enforce harassment policies.

DEFINING SEXUAL HARASSMENT

Harassment is defined as any unwanted, deliberate, or repeated unsolicited comments, gestures, graphic materials, physical contacts, or solicitation of favors based upon one's group membership (employment location). Harassment is illegal in the workplace based upon state and federal equal rights laws.

These laws are as follows:

1. Civil Rights Act of 1964

2. The Age Discrimination In Employment Act

3. The Federal Rehabilitation Act of 1973

4. Several state laws

Sexual harassment is sexual attention imposed on someone who is not in a position to refuse it. Although men can be victims of sexual harassment, most victims are women. Between 40 percent and 90 percent of working women surveyed have identified themselves as victims of sexual harassment.

Harassment occurs when insults, slurs, or other verbal or physical conduct:

• Have the purpose or effect of creating an intimidating, hostile, or offensive employment environment;

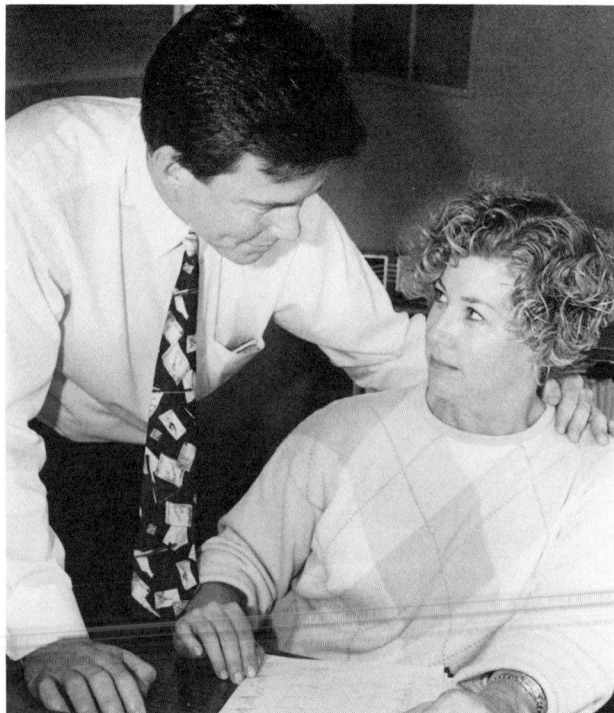

Standing too close to another individual may be viewed as uncomfortable, overly casual, and in some instances, sexually harassing. Avoid hurting yourself and others by keeping a comfortable distance. (Photo by Mary Langenfeld.)

- Have the purpose or effect of unreasonable interference with an individual's academic or employment performance;

- Adversely affect an individual's employment progress or promotion;

Specific examples of improper behavior, words, or gestures in the workplace must be identified. You may think, "What is wrong with this type of joke?" or "A little humor is good for the soul," or "I do not understand why this behavior is wrong," or you may have been brought up in a family environment or another work environment where the behavior may have been acceptable. However, in the current work environment the behavior examples listed in Figure 8.3 are inappropriate and are considered harassment by state and federal law. Loss of one's job and a potential lawsuit are concerns all employees should have.

SEXUAL HARASSMENT IN THE WORKPLACE

- Whistling or cat-calling
- Vulgar and obscene jokes
- Crude or vulgar language
- Pinching or patting
- Unwelcome hugging
- Grabbing or tearing someone's clothing
- Leering or "undressing" the person with your eyes
- Pressuring someone to sit on your knee, hug you, kiss you
- Leaning over someone for a "better view"
- Commenting on the clothing of an individual in a sexual way (example, "Boy, I sure like the way those pants fit.")
- Jokes or comments that put women or men down
- Recounting one's sexual exploits in the office or work area
- Repeatedly asking someone for a date after you have been turned down
- Displaying crude jokes and pictures, including pinups from magazines
- Revealing parts of your body that violate common decency
- Starting and spreading rumors about the sex life of a fellow employee or student
- Physically forcing sexual activity on someone

(Source: Wisconsin Indianhead Technical College Student Handbook)

Figure 8-3. Sexual Harassment in the Workplace

WHAT YOU CAN DO ABOUT SEXUAL HARASSMENT

If harassment is not dealt with by you and/or the employer, it will probably continue and escalate. Bad habits as they relate to sexual harassment may be hard to break and a firm stance is a must. Obviously, you want to work in a warm and friendly environment that is conducive to good working conditions.

Figure 8.4 provides a suggestion of steps you can follow if you think you are being harassed. However, each company may have its own procedures.

Procedure One: **Individual Confrontation**
Confront the person doing the harassment. Let the harasser know what behavior you object to. If it continues, make notes giving specific details of what has taken place. You may need your notes to add credibility to your story.

Procedure Two: **Formal Grievance**
You can file a formal complaint, usually to an affirmative action officer or whoever is in the personnel office. Sometimes companies require that a grievance be filed within a certain number of days. A grievance form is usually available at the personnel office.

Procedure Three: **Follow-up Investigation**
Usually there will be investigations and meetings held to resolve the problem. If the problem is not solved to the mutual satisfaction of all parties involved, then you can appeal or go to procedure four.

Procedure Four: **Lawsuit**
Although this may be the last resort, you may need to contact an attorney and proceed with a lawsuit. Chances are the lawyer will ask you if you followed the above procedures.

Figure 8-4. Steps to Follow When Confronting Harassment

SUMMARY

Work ethics are standards of conduct and moral judgment that you exhibit on the job. These ethics are learned sometimes from various sources: religion, parents, culture, environment, friends, and/or environmental influences. Good work ethics can mean job success and success for your company. Decisions must be made based upon good moral character.

Harassment is related to ethics because it depends on your behavior toward fellow workers or customers. Based on federal and state law, it is illegal in the workplace. Sexual harassment is sexual attention in the form of comments, gestures, graphic materials, physical contact, and favor solicitation that is imposed upon someone who is not in a position to refuse it.

This chapter was included in this book to give you a perspective of what employers expect when it comes to an ethical work environment. If you are unsure about your ethics, you may want to do some more reading or seek help from a counselor.

Some key points to remember:

- **The importance of ethics:** This includes keeping your job, developing a good reputation as a trusted employee, and building upon a successful career.

- **Ethics defined:** In the workplace, ethics relate to codes of conduct that include honesty, trust, legal behavior, and decent treatment of others. Proper ethical behavior can be challenged and confusing, but the definition should direct the right behavior.

- **Ethical issues and correct behavior:** This behavior addresses the proper use of sick days, only using supplies for company business, submitting proper expense accounts, presenting product facts, only using your work time for company business, hiring the best qualified candidate, appropriate licensing of software, gossip avoidance, confidentiality, fairness, and drug and alcohol abstention.

- **Sexual harassment is illegal:** This type of behavior can cost you your job and a possible lawsuit against you.
- **Harassment confrontation procedures:** This procedure includes letting the harasser know what you object to, filing a formal grievance, investigation, and possible lawsuit.

QUESTIONS FOR REVIEW AND DISCUSSION

1. Nicole is one of your best customers. At Christmas she gives you an expensive gift, which is against company policy. If you refuse, you think it will offend her. What should you do?

_____

_____

_____

2. You work in a payroll office and you have been noticing that Darcy, a fellow office worker, takes a sick day about the same time every month—just about the time the payroll work is at its peak. Should you ignore it, talk to Darcy, or talk to the office manager?

_____

_____

_____

3. Sarah went on the same business trip you did. Sarah gives you her expense account and tells you to pad your expense account so that hers does not look high and out of line. She tells you not to worry because everyone does it. How are you going to handle this situation?

_____

_____

_____

4. Mark is a vacuum cleaner salesman. His fellow sales persons have told him that the best sales technique they use is to tell their customers that the vacuum cleaner retails at $599 and for that price they will throw in a floor cleaner at half price for $150. The price $749 is about twice the cost price. Is Mark justified in using this technique?

_____

_____

_____

5. Forrest is an accountant with a CPA firm. When he has time during the day, he uses company time and equipment to do his sports club's books. He is the club's treasurer. You are Forrest's supervisor. What should you do or not do?

_____

_____

_____

6. Good work ethics are related to good moral values. How does sexual harassment violate good moral values?

_____

_____

7. Kewal is a microcomputer expert at a local industry. He is in charge of loading all the new software the company purchases. Kewal has a computer at home. One of his colleagues tells him to copy the software for his home computer because no one would ever know. Please comment.

_____

_____

8. Sexual harassment could be related to the harasser's religion, culture, or parents. This excuse does not make it right. Please explain.

_____

_____

9. You were just verbally harassed on the job in the lunch room for the first time. You tell the offender in front of everyone that he will be hearing from your lawyer and you storm off. What is wrong with this scene?

_____

_____

10. Asha, a fellow employee, comes to you and asks for advice. She thinks some of the male workers could be harassing her when she walks by their desk. What questions should you ask Asha to determine if she is being harassed? If she is, what should Asha do?

_____

_____

CASE STUDY

In Wisconsin, like many other states, you can visit certain areas where Ole and Swen jokes are abundant. In other sections of the state you can hear Polish, Irish, Jewish, and other ethnic humor and stories. Some of the humor is considered clean, and some of the humor is pretty dirty. Is ethnic humor allowable in the workplace? If it is, when does it become offensive? When would it fall under harassment? Who determines if it is offensive? After answering these questions, find a humorous ethnic joke or story. Write it down and insert your ethnic background into the joke or story. What is your reaction? Now write the joke in a way that it would not offend any ethnic group and still be humorous.

PROJECT

Several companies have ethics policies and have developed what is called a "Code of Ethics." Try to obtain a sample code and use this code to develop a code of ethics for your school or business. Use some of the work ethics principles explained in this chapter.

APPENDIX 1

THE PSYCHOLOGY OF CHANGE

By Ronni Sandroff

Just a nanosecond ago, dealing with changes at work was merely a matter of learning new skills—planning in *Lotus,* creating in virtual reality, working at the speed of fax. None of it was easy, but it didn't require that we retool the most basic element in the workplace: ourselves.

Now, to qualify (and continuously requalify) for a place on the workplace team, many of us require an overhaul of our psyches. We need to unlearn basic assumptions, including how we relate to supervisors, colleagues, customers and the very idea of a career. The goal: to transform ourselves into quick-change artists who can turn on a dime, shrug off past successes and failures and frequently reinvent ourselves to fill the new roles that suddenly replace the old.

The new corporate roller-coaster ride creates confusion and disorientation at all levels. Many midlevel executives, professionals and business owners, reeling from the changes in their fields, don't even know the changes in their fields, don't even know what's causing their problems. A pharmaceutical-marketing VP who has built her career by formulating expensive "doctor give-away" projects is abruptly told that the American Medical Association will no longer permit such gifts. A sales chief in the garment industry watches the competition succeed with a bold new approach, but can't convince her company to change. A previously successful private-practice psychologist finds her earnings in steep decline because of changes in health-insurance reimbursements rules. These people lament that they've chosen the wrong industry, the wrong company, the wrong profession, unaware that today—when even the U.S. Army talks of layoffs—there are no safe havens, no stable industries, no occupational ranks in which business as usual still suffices.

The old standby management tactic, which worked well for decades, was simply to push harder when the going got tough: work longer hours, squeeze more from the work force, make everyone come in over the weekend to finish a project. Today the challenge for management is to find innovative new ways to increase their employees' change threshold—and their own. "The secret to mastering greater levels of change is not to press harder on a pedal already floored, but to shift gears," says psychologist and business consultant Daryl Conner, author of *Managing at the Speed of Change.*

Many of the faces of change have long been predicted: the paperless office, the increasingly diverse work force, tightening the reins on medical costs, management by team, outsourcing, JIT (just-in-time) manufacturing. But until the recession and increasing global competition made them a survival necessity, most top managers resisted these changes.

No surprise. With monumental change flooding the workplace, the "future shock" that Alvin Toffler predicted over 20 years ago is officially upon us, and it has some decidedly uncomfortable physiological and psychological components. It starts mildly, with what Toffler called the "orientation response," similar to a dog's pricking up its ears. We try to make sense of the unsettling messages—rumors of layoffs, restructuring, reengineering. Our senses become more acute. Muscles tense. Veins and arteries constrict (thus cold feet and hands) as blood rushes to the brain. Tremors and surges of anticipatory energy pulse through the body. These physiological changes heighten our senses and allow us to take in more information.

Then, as choices, changes and disruptions continue to mount, the state of red alert takes its toll. We begin to retreat into fatigue, apathy and irritability. The stressed psyche becomes vulnerable to replaying old fears and insecurities, causing a kind of mental meltdown of self-confidence. Poor decision-making, reduced trust, decreased honesty and directness, reduced propensity for risk-taking and a tendency to vent job frustrations at home are common side effects, according to studies conducted by Conner. As the stakes rise and confusion grows, these stress symptoms come to include such severe dysfunctional reactions as malicious compliance (doing only what is absolutely necessary), chronic depression, addictive behaviors and overt as well as covert undermining of the company.

Even if the change is positive, shifting gears too rapidly can leave skid marks on the brain. Often, the individual blames herself or her particular situation for the stress symptoms, not realizing that she is part of a national, even global, syndrome.

Drastic change is particularly hard on the middle-aged and middle ranks in corporations, studies have found. The young, low-level worker has little to lose from change, unless she's actually fired. And many senior workers have had a chance to assemble a well-stocked life raft in case they suddenly need to jump ship. But the vast group of baby-boomers in their late 30s to 50s have invested a lot in learning to play the game. They don't want the rules to change, because they haven't yet received the promised payoff. The all-bets-are-off atmosphere is not only very upsetting, it requires enormous energy just to stay functional, let alone thrive.

Conner has devised a workplace-resilience test that measures component qualities he has personally observed in his consulting work. These include social and mental flexi-

143

bility ("Sometimes one new piece of information will completely change how I see a situation"), focus ("My life has direction and purpose"), proactivity, organization and a positive view of oneself and the world ("When times are tough, I focus my attention on a brighter tomorrow"). A great deal more research is needed to find out whether these are indeed the qualities that help individuals bounce and, if so, whether they can be successfully taught. Meanwhile, the best bet for thriving in today's atmosphere of change is to imitate the methods of successfully resilient people.

THE ENTHUSIASM EDGE

The change experts agree on one thing: The positive attitude of resilient people is their most potent survival skill. When sifting through employees, managers retain the ones who make them feel good, who maintain an upbeat, energetic attitude when everyone else is in a state of collapse. Often these are people who recover very quickly from a fear of failure in a new situation.

"Almost everyone feels afraid when they're asked to change. It's what you do with the fear that counts," notes publishing consultant Nancy Woodhull, who helps her clients shift focus to attract a wider female audience. "Some reporters and editors turn the fear that they'll be incapable of meeting the new demands into a denial that change is necessary. The reporter who's told to do fewer football and more women's-interest stories should not try to convince the boss that the shift isn't necessary," counsels Woodhull. In her experience, reporters who quicky accept the need to adapt in order to meet the changing market soon find ways to acquire the new skills they need to succeed.

Fortunately, adopting a positive attitude does not mean adopting a rosy world view—a difficult feat for people trained in critical thinking— but avoiding overly negative interpretations of disruptive change: "This is a catastrophe"; "This means I'll never work again"; "I'm a total failure"; "Everything I do gets screwed up"; "I should never have entered this field."

"Ask yourself: Is there any less destructive way to look at this change?" recommends psychologist Martin Seligman of the University of Pennsylvania, the author of *Learned Optimism,* a popular book among management consultants. "Looking for evidence of a more positive, less catastrophic view of some change helps you find the energy to take the next steps."

This technique, which some psychologists call "reframing," can be profoundly effective. While all change involves loss, it also opens up new opportunities for gain. "Those who succeed in times of chaos manage to turn the situation inside out and find some personal advantages in it," says Ellen Langer. At the very least, change adds some excitement to life and relieves you of the naive expectation that the workplace will remain stable.

TOUCHSTONE VALUES

Along with mental flexibility and practice in surviving change, resilient people demonstrate a willingness to mold their own sense of identity. When work lives were more predictable, it wasn't so risky for an individual to measure herself by title and position. "I'm a product manager at a Fortune 100 company" was a personal calling card as well as a job description.

But what if major changes occur: your company starts to slip, or you're laid off, or all the product managers are told they now report to each other? "Today we have to learn to place our ideals and sense of value somewhere else so we're not faced with a tremendous loss of self when job identity is taken away," says management consultant Robert Bramson, author of *Coping With the Fast Track Blues.*

Where is that somewhere else? Bramson recommends that professionals cultivate a "guild mentality," similar to that of the Renaissance, in which workers identified with the values, standards and skills represented by their professional organizations. A worker's standing in the guild transcended his relationship with any particular job.

"If you know what your core abilities and values are, career changes don't seem so threatening," says psychologist turned CEO Marlene Piturro. "My touchstone value is ex-

pertise—I know how to become an expert in many different areas."

Speaking both as a psychologist and someone who's gone through several career changes, Piturro believes it's important for every [woman] to identify her core values. "It may be helping people, making scientific discoveries, exercising creativity or being part of something that matters," says Piturro. "If you're not sure what your key values are, explore and find out. Once you do, change won't seem so menacing, because you take your core abilities and values wherever you go."

21ST-CENTURY CAREER PLANS

Employees at companies that are embracing and managing change in a positive way can consider themselves fortunate. Participating in such transformations may be a more valuable part of the résumé of the future than any specific job skills.

Stedt, an executive vice president of travel-related services at American Express, expects to look for enthusiasm and resilience when she hires in the future: "We're no longer interested only in the straight-A student. He or she might crumble when faced with a setback or a sudden change." Well-rounded people who can derive pleasure from many areas may be better suited to solving the company's problems. "We'll look for people who *like* to deal with ambiguity, who don't need structure or a defined job," says Stedt. "Because the job is bound to change. Maybe in 24 hours you'll experience a change of boss, organization, job design, the way you're evaluated. Even compensation for middle managers might be judged differently. Not only what you do but how you do it may change. We need people who can survive this and still enjoy their work."

Being flexible does not mean you have to abandon all your long-term career plans and goals. But the new type of plans have to have built-in expectations of further change. "In this economy, most high achievers will find themselves maxing out in corporations between the ages of 45 and 60," predicts Piturro. "We just become too expensive. So we all need to do some dreaming and formulate a general plan for what we want to do later on—a consulting or entrepreneurial move." Then, when convulsions hit your workplace, you're not starting from scratch when you contemplate what's next.

Sometimes, staying flexible means ignoring sage career advice from the past. When Nancy Woodhull left her corporate-news career at media giants Gannett and Time to become a consultant, she was concerned that she had arranged no detailed business plan: "Most people put together a plan and work it. These plans are usually so straight-ahead, they don't leave any room for things as they change." Instead, Woodhull decided to explore the territory and let her business evolve over time. "I said, 'Here's the river I want to float on, here's the direction I want to go,' and put my boat on it. I was ready for the river to take unexpected turns and present obstacles."

Woodhull's general idea was to become a consultant on marketing to women, and she soon found that the overwhelming majority of her clients were newspaper and television executives. Now she successfully specializes in teaching media clients how to rejigger their formats in order to appeal to female audiences.

Perhaps the most important thing for workers at all levels to do is to let go of the expectation that they can adequately predict the future. Forget the career ladder, with its expectations of an orderly acquisition of skills and regular promotions. As Woodhull suggests, it's more useful to visualize career planning as steering your ship down an unexplored river. The journey requires attentiveness to evolving conditions, the ability to stay on course—and a well-developed taste for surviving by your wits.

Source: WORKING WOMAN JULY 1993. Reprinted with permission.

GIVING GOOD ANSWERS TO TOUGH INTERVIEW QUESTIONS

By Claire McIntosh

You are sailing through your interview for the perfect job. Then trouble strikes: The interviewer catches you off guard with a sensitive or personal question. Your first impulse may be to say, "That's none of your business," but a better strategy is to redirect the conversation without appearing adversarial. If the question is job related, experts suggest you answer it. And keep in mind that questions about money, family, drug use, lapses on your record or any other aspect of your personal life have to be handled with care. The following are some of the toughest—and most common—interview questions you will encounter. We asked two career experts for the best answers to get you out of the hot seat and into the job of your choice.

"WHY HAVE YOU CHANGED JOBS SO FREQUENTLY?"

"EXPERTS USED to predict that the average person would have four jobs in a lifetime. Now, because of social, economic and technological changes, the average person is likely to have four *careers*," says Martin John Yate, author of *Knock 'Em Dead: With Great Answers to Tough Interview Questions*. Frequent job changes may be common, but they're still frowned upon. Make sure you have an acceptable reason for leaving each job, such as to gain more challenge, security, money or advancement, or to shorten a lengthy commute. You also want to be certain the interviewer knows that your job hopping was never a result of disloyalty or poor performance, and that you grew professionally with each job change. "Say something like, 'I moved as opportunities to broaden my experience came up. Now I want to settle down and make my diverse background pay off in my contribution to my new employer,' " recommends Yate. "I used this personally to explain some rather unusual job changes, and it worked," he adds.

"WHY WERE YOU OUT OF WORK FOR SO LONG?"

"YOU MUST have a sound explanation for any gaps in your employment history," says Yate. Taking time off to care for a child or an ailing parent is common among working women these days and is a perfectly acceptable explanation, according to Phyllis Martin, author of *Martin's Magic Formula for Getting the Right Job*. If you spent two years writing a novel or going back to college, say so, and emphasize how the experience might benefit the employer. However, "a stay at a mental-health or substance-abuse treatment center is none of the interviewer's business," says Martin. If you can't give a more straightforward explanation for your hiatus, "emphasize that you were not just looking for another paycheck—that you were looking for a company where you could enjoy your work and make a long-term contribution," says Yate.

"WHY WERE YOU FIRED?"

"BEING FIRED is no longer the stigma that it used to be. Eight out of ten people will be terminated at some point in their career," says Yate. Simply give a straight-forward explanation, such as, "I was one of 200 employers who were laid off when my company was taken over by XYZ Corporation. I was employed there for five years, and gained a great deal of experience that could benefit your company." If you were fired for a mistake you made, admit it. "Then emphasize what you learned from the experience and how that knowledge will benefit your next employer," adds Martin. Most important, refrain from bad-mouthing your former employer.

"WHAT IS YOUR SALARY REQUIREMENT?"

WHEN ASKED about your salary requirement, you don't want to show your hand first and risk getting low-balled. Yate suggests throwing the ball back into the interviewer's court: "I am sure that if I'm the best person for the job, you'll make me a fair offer. What figure did you have in mind?" If he asks about your present salary, say something like, "I am earning in the 20s, but the market salary for the position you're interviewing me for is between $30,00 and $35,000, and I now have experience comparable to a person in this position."

"DO YOU HAVE YOUNG CHILDREN?"

SINCE EMPLOYERS are often wary of hiring mothers, who they fear might take too much time away from the office, many women are justifiably hesitant to answer questions about children. Yate suggests handling such questions by addressing the concern behind them. When asked if you have young children or if you are planning a family, say, "That's a personal matter, but if you're concerned that my outside obligations might interfere with my schedule, let me say that I understand this position requires long hours and travel, and I am prepared to handle that." If you want to mention your children, go ahead, but be sure to establish your dependability by mentioning that you have reliable child care or by citing your consistent work record.

"ARE YOU WILLING TO BE DRUG TESTED?"

IN THIS CASE, there's only one correct answer if you want the job—a cheerful "yes," says Yate. In many cases, that alone will be enough to reassure the employer, and they won't administer a test. But if they do, be sure to find out what type of tests they are using and which foods or medications could trigger a false positive.

WHEN A QUESTION IS UNFAIR

Before you answer *any* question, it's important to recognize whether or not it's fair. "Fair questions are questions that are job related and that cannot be used for discriminatory purposes," says Martin. For instance, if you apply for work as a paralegal for an immigration lawyer, an interviewer may ask if you speak Spanish, but not whether it's your native tongue.

Your interviewer is almost certainly going to know the difference—that any inquiry that forces you to reveal your race, nationality, age, religion or marital status is discriminatory. But if she or he makes a gaffe and asks you such a question, should you ever take your chances and answer it? Surprisingly, Yate says yes. According to him, the majority of interviewers don't intend to discriminate—they are only showing a friendly, though misguided, interest. But if you're unsure about the interviewer's motives, don't risk it. To brush off the question without brushing off the interviewer, Yate suggests blaming his mistake on the company. "Simply reply—with eyebrows raised in surprise—'In view of the fair-employment laws, I'm surprised your company would require you to ask me that. I hope you'll understand if I decline to answer.' " Be friendly, not accusatory, or you'll make the interviewer uncomfortable. And who wants to hire someone who makes them feel uneasy?

Before your next interview, try to anticipate any sensitive issues that might be raised. Then personalize your responses, and rehearse them in a way that sounds most natural for you. Finessing your way through the toughest of interview questions doesn't merely keep you in the running for the position, it demonstrates to employers that you have the ability to handle pressure and the know-how to turn a potential obstacle into an opportunity.

Source: McCall's, May 1991. Reprinted with permission.

Glossary

ADVERTISEMENT. Commonly called classified or want ads in publications like the local newspaper.

BOND. An insurance policy that protects employers from financial loss caused by their employees.

CARRIER CREATIVITY. The ability to come up with professional processes and methods to get an interview and land a job.

CAREER INITIATIVE. The ability to be proactive in seeking out potential employers.

CAREER PLAN. The individual ideas, objectives and goals that you develop, organize and implement to satisfy your career aspirations.

CHRONOLOGICAL RESUME. More traditional and focused on the position and employer. It lists education and employment history in chronological order.

COLD CANVASS. When you don't have prior knowledge of any job openings, you canvass employers by sending out a cover letter and resume with the hope that someone can use your talents and experience.

COMBINATION RESUME. A combination of the chronological and functional resume.

COVER LETTER. A business letter sent with the resume to an employer requesting consideration for a specific position with the organization.

CUSTOMER SERVICE. Treating customers with respect, meeting their needs and wants, and doing it in a friendly manner.

DICTIONARY OF OCCUPATIONAL TITLES. A reference work providing comprehensive career information, including working conditions, training, and education requirements for a wide variety of occupations.

ENTREPRENEURS. Individuals who own their own business.

EQUAL EMPLOYMENT OPPORTUNITY (EEO). A company policy meaning employers do not practice any kind of discrimination.

EEO SURVEY. A questionnaire employers use to determine whether minorities or veterans are applying for employment with their company.

ETHICS. Moral principles or codes of conduct by which people should conduct their daily lives.

FUNCTIONAL RESUME. A resume focusing on skills and achievements rather than the specific positions/employers that you have had.

GOODS PRODUCING OCCUPATIONS. Jobs that produce products, such as manufacturing, mining and agricultural goods.

JOB INTERVIEW. The formal meeting between a job applicant and a representative of an organization.

LETTER OF INQUIRY. A letter used to inquire about the possibility of a job opening when you don't know if any vacancy exists.

NETWORKING. Connecting with people or groups so they can assist you in obtaining a job.

OCCUPATIONAL OUTLOOK HANDBOOK. A handbook that reviews issues and trends for a wide variety of jobs in all occupational areas.

PERFORMANCE EVALUATION. The process an organization uses to determine how well employees are doing their job.

PROFESSIONAL OCCUPATIONS. Jobs that usually require an advanced education, such as lawyers, doctors, accountants and engineers.

RESUME. An organized outline of information that is relative to your getting the job you want.

SERVICE OCCUPATIONS. Jobs that provide services like banking, real estate, education, health care and computer information services.

SEXUAL HARASSMENT. Sexual attention imposed on someone who is not in a position to refuse it.

TECHNICAL OCCUPATIONS. Jobs that require more than a high school education, but less than a four-year college degree, such as legal assistant, x-ray technician, dental hygienist and auto body repair technician.

THANK-YOU LETTER. A kind and conscientious effort on your part to express your gratitude to an employer for granting you an interview.

TOTAL QUALITY MANAGEMENT (TQM). A process that involves the team approach to plan, organize and implement quality in the development of goods and services.

Index